lonely planet

POCKET

CHICAGO

TOP SIGHTS · LOCAL EXPERIENCES

ALI LEMER, KARLA ZIMMERMAN

Contents

Plan Your Trip   4

Gourmet Chicago hot dog
PRAIRIE_EYE/GETTY IMAGES ©

Explore Chicago 31

Worth a Trip

Survival Guide 147

Special Features

Welcome to Chicago

Take cloud-scraping architecture, lakefront beaches and world-class museums, stir in wild comedy, fret-bending guitar music and very hefty pizza, and you've got a town that won't let you down. The city center is a steely wonder, but it's Chicago's mural-splashed neighborhoods – with their inventive world-cuisine restaurants, fringe theaters and sociable dive bars – that really blow you away.

Top Sights

Art Institute of Chicago
Marble halls filled with masterpieces. **p38**

VENI/GETTY IMAGES ©

Willis Tower

Views from Chicago's loftiest skyscraper. **p40**

RAY LASKOWITZ/LONELY PLANET ©

Lincoln Park

Chicago's biggest park and playground. **p82**

FILEDIMAGE/SHUTTERSTOCK ©

Wrigley Field

Iconic ballpark full of tradition. **p96**

Field Museum of Natural History
All-encompassing museum. **p130**

360° Chicago
Panoramas high in the sky. **p68**

Millennium Park
Park with whimsical public art. **p34**

Robie House
Frank Lloyd Wright's Prairie-style masterwork. **p144**

Museum of Science & Industry

Diverse science museum. **p142**

Navy Pier

Carnival on the wharf with a 3300ft-long pier. **p56**

LEFT: JOE HENDRICKSON/SHUTTERSTOCK ©
RIGHT: HENRYK SADURA/GETTY IMAGES ©

PETER MCCULLOUGH, © MCA CHICAGO

Museum of Contemporary Art (MCA)

Audacious, thought-provoking museum. **p70**

Eating

Chicago is a chowhound's hot spot. For the most part, restaurants here are reasonably priced and pretension-free, serving masterful food in come-as-you-are environs. You can also fork into a superb range of international eats, especially if you break out of downtown and head for neighborhoods such as Pilsen or Andersonville.

Local Specialties

Foremost is deep-dish pizza, with crust that rises two or three inches above the plate and cradles a molten pile of toppings. One gooey piece is practically a meal. Also iconic is the Chicago hot dog – a wiener in a poppy-seed bun with myriad toppings (including onions, tomatoes, a dill pickle and neon-green relish) – but never ketchup). The city is also revered for its spicy, drippy, only-in-Chicago Italian beef sandwiches.

Eat Streets

Chicago's best and brightest chefs cook on Randolph St in the West Loop. Copious sidewalk seating spills out of hip bistros and cafes on Division St in Wicker Park. Mexican taquerias meet hipster hangouts along 18th St in Pilsen.

Best for Foodies

Alinea Molecular gastronomy at one of the world's best restaurants. (p91)

Girl & the Goat Rockin' ambience and dishes starring the titular animal. (p124)

Smyth Two Michelin stars for seasonal comfort food, with ingredients from the restaurant's farm. (p125)

Revival Food Hall A slew of all-local, hipster eats to choose from. (p49)

Best Budget

Lou Mitchell's Route 66 diner where waitstaff call you 'honey' without irony. (p124)

Irazu Chicago's lone Costa Rican eatery whips up distinctive, peppery fare. (p109)

Publican Quality Meats Beefy sandwiches straight from the butcher's block. (p122)

SHINYSHOT/SHUTTERSTOCK ©

Best Pizza

Giordano's It's like deep-dish on steroids, with awesomely bulked-up crusts. (p63)

Pizano's Makes a great thin crust to supplement the deep dish. (p50)

Best Vegan

Chicago Diner Chicago's long-standing all-veg linchpin. (p99)

Native Foods Cafe World-ranging plant-based menu accompanied by organic beers and wines. (p49)

Best Brunch

Sweet Maple Cafe Fresh-baked biscuits and banana pancakes. (p122)

Big Jones Dishes from New Orleans and the Carolina Lowcountry. (p103)

Best Sweets

Hoosier Mama Pie Company Supreme flaky goodness. (p108)

Margie's Candies Gigantic hot fudge sundaes. (p109)

Best Mexican

Topolobampo/ Frontera Grill Rick Bayless'

flavor-packed signature restaurants. (p63)

Don Pedro Carnitas Authentic Pilsen haunt for the city's best tacos. (p138)

Best Hot Dogs

Hot 'G' Dog Goes beyond gourmet weenies, with a killer Chicago-style dog too. (p103)

Wieners Circle Char-dogs, cheddar fries and lots of unruly swearing. (p90)

Dining Out

Make dinner reservations for eateries in mid-range and upper price brackets, especially on weekends. Many restaurants let you book online

Drinking & Nightlife

Chicagoans love to hang out in drinking establishments. Blame it on the long winter, when folks need to huddle together somewhere warm. Blame it on summer, when sunny days make beer gardens and sidewalk patios so splendid. Whatever the reason, drinking in the city is a widely cherished civic pastime.

Dance Clubs

Clubs cluster in three main areas: River North and West Loop, where the venues tend to be huge and luxurious, with dress codes; Wicker Park and Ukrainian Village, where they're typically more casual; and Wrigleyville and Boystown, where they fall somewhere in between. Most clubs use social media to provide discounts on admission, so check before heading out.

How to Find a Real Chicago Bar

To discover classic, character-filled bars on your own, look for the following: an Old Style or Hamm's beer sign swinging out front; a well-worn dartboard and/or pool table inside; patrons wearing ballcaps with the logos of the Cubs, White Sox, Bears or Blackhawks; and sports on TV.

Best Vibes

Old Town Ale House Trendy tipplers and grizzled regulars sip under bawdy paintings. (p91)

RM Champagne Salon Twinkling West Loop spot that feels like a Parisian cafe. (p126)

Best Beer

Revolution Brewing Industrial-chic brewpub pouring righteous ales. (p115)

Centennial Crafted Beer & Eatery Warm beer bar with 50 taps. (p64)

Delilah's Spirited punk bar with all kinds of odd ales (and whiskeys too). (p91)

Best Cocktails

Violet Hour Beard Award–winning cocktails in a hidden bar. (p111)

MASSIMO BORCHI/ATLANTIDE PHOTOTRAVEL/GETTY IMAGES ©

Sparrow Bespoke rum-based concoctions in a cozy retro bar. (p78)

Lost Lake Cool, refreshing tiki concoctions. (p115)

Best Wine

Bar Ramone Sparkling nightcap in a European-style salon. (p64)

Press Room Reds and whites in a candlelit basement. (p127)

Best Views

Waydown Cocktails and skyscraper views atop the Ace Hotel. (p126)

Signature Lounge Ascend to the Hancock Center's 96th floor and gawp. (p69)

Cindy's Loop rooftop with vistas of Millennium Park. (p51)

Best Clubs

Smart Bar Intimate club that's serious about its DJs. (p100)

Berlin Welcome-one, welcome-all space to dance your ass off. (p101)

Best Local Bars

Skylark Where Pilsen's underground goes for cheap drinks and tater tots. (p140)

Innertown Pub Authentic kitsch and cheap drinks tucked away in Ukrainian Village. (p111)

Ten Cat Tavern Shoot pool, check out the art and swill beers by the fireplace. (p100)

Bar & Club Events

The Chicago Reader (www.chicagoreader.com) has bar and club listings. The drinking age is 21 years. Take your driver's license or passport out at night: you will be asked for ID.

Shopping

From the glossy department stores of the Magnificent Mile to the indie designers of Wicker Park, Chicago is a shopper's destination. It has been that way from the get-go. After all, this is the city that birthed the department store and traditions such as the money-back guarantee, bridal registry and bargain basement.

Specialties

Music is big. Independent record stores flood Chicago's neighborhoods, supported by the thriving live-music scene in town. Vinyl geeks will find heaps of stacks to flip through. Vintage and thrift fashions are another claim to fame. Folks here don't throw out their old bowling shirts, pillbox hats, faux-fur coats and costume jewelry. Instead, they deposit used duds at vintage or secondhand stores, of which there are heaps. Art- and architecture-related items are another Chicago specialty.

Locally Made Wares

Several stores proffer handbags, pendants, dresses and journals that city artisans have stitched, sewed and glue-gunned themselves. You're pretty much guaranteed a one-of-a-kind item to take home.

Best Music

Reckless Records Great place to get the scoop on local indie rock bands. (p112)

Dave's Records *Rolling Stone* magazine dubbed it one of the nation's best stores. (p93)

Dusty Groove Killer stacks of vinyl hold rare soul and funk beats. (pictured; p113)

Best Books

Quimby's Ground zero for comics, zines and underground culture. (p112)

Pilsen Community Books Charming shop with floor-to-ceiling books. (p140)

Open Books Welcoming used bookstore with a whopping selection. (p127)

Best Souvenirs

Chicago Architecture Center Shop Pick up a mini Willis Tower model or skyline poster. (p53)

KAMIL KRZACZYNSKI/AFP/GETTY IMAGES ©

Transit Tees Creative Chicago logo designs found on anything you can imagine. (p113)

Art Institute of Chicago Posters and note cards of the collection's masterpieces. (p38)

Best Fashion & Vintage

Una Mae's Emerge looking all Jackie O in your new old hat. (p113)

Knee Deep Vintage Groovy garb from the 1920s to the 1970s. (p141)

Best Arts & Crafts

Randolph Street Market Its Indie Designer Market is the epicenter of Chicago craftiness. (p127)

Andersonville Galleria Three floors of local indie vendors. (p103)

ShopColumbia Goods from Columbia College's arty students. (p53)

Pilsen Outpost Artist-run gallery with unique T-shirts, posters and paintings for sale. (p141)

Best for Kids

American Girl Place Have tea and get a new hairdo with your doll. (p79)

Lego Store So many cool things to build at the hands-on tables. (p79)

Rotofugi Quirky and inventive items at an unconventional toy store. (p93)

Deals & Openings

Chicago magazine (www.chicagomag.com) publishes a roundup of sales and new store openings on a weekly basis via its 'sales check' newsletter. Sales tax on goods (excluding food) is 10.25%.

Architecture

The Great Fire of 1871 sparked an architectural revolution in Chicago. It created a blank slate where new ideas could be tested. Daniel Burnham, one of the prime designers during the era, encouraged architects to think big and not be put off by traditional limits. The city has been a hotbed for skyscraper design ever since.

Notable Names

Louis Sullivan was Chicago's architectural founding father, a revolutionary of steel-frame highrises. His student Frank Lloyd Wright catapulted the Prairie style to global renown. Daniel Burnham was the man with the plan that preserved Chicago's lakefront. Ludwig Mies van der Rohe created simple, boxy designs for modern skyscrapers. Jeanne Gang, Chicago's current starchitect, has mod, organic structures popping up all over the city.

Preservation

The Chicago Architecture Foundation – known today for its great tours and gift shop – grew out of a 1960s preservation effort to save a South Loop home. The group was successful with that building, but many others met the wrecking ball, most famously the Stock Exchange Building, designed by Louis Sullivan and Dankmar Adler. The Stock Exchange Arch was salvaged and now stands outside the Art Institute (on the northeast side). Several groups have since sprung up to ensure Chicago's worthy buildings live on.

Best Skyscrapers

Willis Tower Ascend 103 floors, then peer straight down from a glass-floored ledge in Chicago's tallest building. (p40)

Aqua Tower Jeanne Gang's 86-story beauty has won numerous awards for its dramatic, wavy design. (p46)

875 N Michigan Ave Get high at the lakeside tower's 94th-floor observatory or 96th-floor lounge. (p68)

MABRY CAMPBELL/GETTY IMAGES © ARCHITECT: BERTRAND GOLDBERG

Tribune Tower This neo-Gothic tower is inlaid with stones from the Taj Mahal, Parthenon and more. (p60)

Marina City The groovy corncob towers look like something from a *Jetsons* cartoon. (pictured; p60)

Kluczynski Federal Building Ludwig Mies van der Rohe launched the modern skyscraper look with this boxy structure. (p47)

Best Beaux Arts

Chicago Cultural Center Gilded ceilings, marble walls and mother-of-pearl mosaics deck the halls. (p47)

Museum of Science & Industry It was the classical Palace of Fine Arts at the landmark 1893 World's Expo. (p142)

Best Frank Lloyd Wright

Robie House The graceful lines of Wright's Hyde Park masterpiece were emulated around the world. (p144)

Charnley-Persky House Only 19 years old when he designed it, Wright declared the 11-room abode the first modern building. (p76)

Best Mansions

Driehaus Museum A Gilded Age manor with three floors of gorgeous decorative arts and stained glass. (p60)

Patterson-McCormick Mansion A turn-of-the-century neoclassical home built when Astor St was millionaires' row. (p79)

Worth a Trip

The **Frank Lloyd Wright Home & Studio** (☎312-994-4000; www.flwright.org; 951 Chicago Ave; adult/child $18/15; ☺10am-4pm), in suburban Oak Park, offers a fascinating, hour-long walk-through of the famed architect's abode from 1889 to 1909. It's easy to reach via the Green Line train from downtown Chicago.

Museums & Galleries

The world's largest T rex. The most impressionist paintings outside of France. The Western Hemisphere's biggest science museum. Chicago's superlative institutions draw millions of visitors each year. A fine assortment of smaller venues covers everything from Mexican beadwork to antique medical equipment, plus galleries galore.

Online Tickets

Most museums allow you to buy tickets online. You're assured entry and sometimes even get to skip the regular ticket lines. But there's an occasional service fee ($2 or so), and sometimes the prepay line is almost as long as the regular one. Consider buying online in summer and for big exhibits – otherwise, there's no need.

Gallery Districts

Chicago has five main gallery districts. River North is the most entrenched, where top international names show off their works; it also has the largest concentration of galleries. The West Loop features edgy, avant-garde art that garners international praise. Bucktown and Wicker Park are rife with alternative spaces and emerging talent. Pilsen hosts several small, artist-run spaces with erratic hours. And the South Side neighborhood of Bridgeport has become a player with cool-cat galleries in a warren of old warehouses on W 35th St.

Best for Art

Art Institute of Chicago Gawk at Monets, modern works and much more at the nation's second-largest art museum. (p38)

Museum of Contemporary Art The Art Institute's brash, rebellious sibling has a collection that always pushes boundaries. (p70)

National Museum of Mexican Art Holds a terrific collection of paintings, altars, folk art and politically charged pieces. (p136)

Best for Science

Field Museum of Natural History Explore dinosaurs, gems, mummies and enormous taxidermied lions. (p130)

ZUMA PRESS, INC./ALAMY STOCK PHOTO ©

Museum of Science & Industry The largest science museum in the Western Hemisphere. (p142)

Adler Planetarium Journey to the nether regions of outer space at this lakeside gem. (p136)

Best Galleries

Intuit: The Center for Intuitive & Outsider Art Small museum featuring talented outsider artists. (p108)

Wrightwood 659 Architecture exhibits in a new, Tadao Ando–designed space. (p88)

Mars Gallery Colorful, cartoony pop-art fun in a historic building. (p122)

Best Offbeat

International Museum of Surgical Science Antique equipment and fascinating exhibits on the history of medical science. (p77)

American Writers Museum Engrossing interactive displays on American literature

will absorb book lovers for hours. (pictured; p48)

Chicago History Museum Tells the city's story with artifacts such as Prohibition-era booze stills. (p88)

Money Museum Emerge with a take-home bag of shredded currency and photo with the million-dollar briefcase. (p46)

Worth a Trip

The **Zhou B Art Center** (✆773-523-0200; www.zhoubartcenter.com; 1029 W 35th St, Bridgeport; ⏰main exhibition spaces 10am-5pm Mon-Sat; 🚌8) fills a massive old warehouse with galleries and studios, showing contemporary paintings and sculpture by well-known international artists. Visit during the popular Third Friday Open Studios event (from 7pm to 10pm).

Tours

Chicago offers loads of tours. Boat excursions are the most popular way to go. The skyline takes on a surreal majesty as you float through its shadows on the Chicago River. Jaunts by foot, bus or bicycle are great for exploring neighborhoods or delving into particular topics, such as art deco buildings, gangster sites or breweries.

SHOBEIR ANSARI/GETTY IMAGES ©

Chicago Architecture Center Tours (CAC; ☎312-922-3432; www.architecture.org; 111 E Wacker Dr; tours $20-55) Gold-standard boat and walking tours show off Chicago's architectural splendor.

Chicago Detours (☎312-350-1131; www.chicagodetours.com; tours from $28) Engrossing walking and bus tours take in Chicago's architecture, history and culture.

Chicago by Foot (☎312-612-0826; www.freetoursbyfoot.com) Pay-what-you-want walking tours covering Loop architecture, West Loop history and more.

InstaGreeter (www.chicagogreeter.com/instagreeter; 77 E Randolph St; ⏱10am-3pm Fri & Sat, 11am-2pm Sun; Ⓜ Brown, Orange, Green, Purple, Pink Line to Washington/Wabash) Free, one-hour Loop tours run frequently; no bookings needed.

Chicago Food Planet Tours (☎312-932-0800; www.chicagofoodplanet.com; 2-3hr tours $45-60) Graze through neighborhood eateries around Wicker Park, Chinatown and others.

Weird Chicago Tours (☎217-791-7859; www.weirdchicago.com; 600 N Clark St, River North; 3hr tours $40; Ⓜ Red Line to Grand) Buses swing by ghost, gangster and grisly crime sites.

Windy (☎312-451-2700; www.tallshipwindy.com; 600 E Grand Ave, Navy Pier; 60-75min tours adult/child $30/10; ⏱May-Oct; 🚌65) Four-masted schooner offers a relaxing sail for skyline views.

Tour Discounts

Many companies offer discounts if you book online. Outdoor-oriented tours usually operate from April to November only.

Comedy & Performing Arts

Improv comedy was born in Chicago, and the city still nurtures the best in the biz. Chicago's reputation for stage drama is well deserved, with Hollywood-star-laden Steppenwolf among the 200 local theaters. Many productions export to Broadway; others play in fringy 'off-Loop' storefronts. The symphonies also draw worldwide accolades.

BARRY BRECHEISEN / STRINGER/GETTY IMAGES ©

Improv

US improv started in a Hyde Park bar in 1955 with the Compass Players, who used audience suggestions in their quick-witted routine. They went on to found Second City, and their style of spectator-fueled skits became world famous. Pictured above: comedian Marina Franklin performing in Chicago.

Theater District

Chicago's Theater District is a group of century-old, neon-lit playhouses that cluster at State and Randolph Sts. They usually host big touring productions.

Best Comedy

Second City The legendary improv bastion. (p92)

iO Theater Large improv house with four theaters. (p93)

Best Theater

Steppenwolf Theatre Home of Malkovich and other stars. (p92)

Goodman Theatre Excellent new and classic American plays. (p53)

Best Classical

Grant Park Orchestra Listen and picnic at Pritzker Pavilion. (p52)

Chicago Symphony Orchestra World-renowned orchestra with a smokin' brass section. (p53)

Dramatic Value

Website **Hot Tix** (www.hottix.org) sells same-week drama, comedy and performing-arts tickets for half price (plus a $5 to $10 service charge).

For Kids

STEVEGEER/GETTY IMAGES ©

Ferocious dinosaurs at the Field Museum, an ark's worth of beasts at Lincoln Park Zoo, lakefront boat rides and sandy beaches are among the top choices for toddlin' times. Add in magical playgrounds, family cycling tours and lots of pizza, and it's clear Chicago is a kid's kind of town.

Best Activities

Navy Pier The whirling swing, sky-high Ferris wheel, musical carousel and boats. (p56)

Maggie Daley Park Imaginative playgrounds, plus rock climbing and mini-golf. (pictured; p46)

Lincoln Park Zoo Swinging chimps, roaring lions and a barnyard full of farm animals to feed. (p88)

12th St Beach Pint-sized waves are perfect for pint-sized swimmers. (p137)

Bobby's Bike Hike Rents children's bikes and offers kid-friendly tours. (p150)

Best Museums

Chicago Children's Museum Building, climbing and inventing exhibits keep young ones busy. (p60)

Peggy Notebaert Nature Museum The butterfly haven, bird garden and marsh full of frogs provide gentle thrills. (p89)

Museum of Science & Industry Kids can conduct 'research' in the Idea Factory. (p142)

Field Museum of Natural History The PlayLab lets tykes excavate dinosaur bones. (p130)

Top Tips for Children

For kid-friendly happenings, see *Chicago Parent* (www.chicagoparent.com) and Chicago Kids (www.chicagokids.com). Children under seven ride free on the L train and public buses; those age seven to 11 pay a reduced fare.

Best Eating

RJ Grunts Burgers and milkshakes by the zoo. (p85)

Gino's East Write on the walls while you wait for your pizza. (p63)

LGBT+

Exploring kinky artifacts in the Leather Archives & Museum, or playing a game of naughty Twister at a rollicking street fair? Shopping for gay literature, or clubbing alongside male go-go dancers? Chicago's flourishing gay and lesbian scene in party-hearty Boystown and easygoing Andersonville offers plenty of choices.

ROBERTO GALAN/GETTY IMAGES ©

Festivals

The main event on the calendar is the **Pride Parade** (pictured; www.chicagopride.com), held the last Sunday in June. It winds through Boystown and attracts more than 800,000 revelers. **Northalsted Market Days** (www.northalsted.com), held in Boystown, is a two-day street fair in mid-August. Crafty vendors line Halsted St, but most folks come for the drag queens in feather boas, street-side Twister games and pop divas on the main stage. Late May's **International Mr Leather** (www.imrl.com) contest brings out lots of men in, well, leather. Workshops and parties take place around town; the main event happens at a downtown hotel or theater.

Best Venues

Big Chicks It's often called the friendliest gay bar in Chicago. (p103)

Second Story Cash-only, disco-ball-spinning bar that hides downtown. (p64)

Roscoe's Tavern Boystown stalwart with a casual bar in front and dance club in back. (p101)

Gay Events

o The *Windy City Times* (www.windycitymediagroup.com) is an LGBT newspaper, published weekly. Its website is the main source for events and entertainment.

o For more than three decades **Berlin** (p101) has been where party people dance until the wee hours.

Four Perfect Days

Day 1

BITMI2/SHUTTERSTOCK ©

Take a boat or walking tour with the **Chicago Architecture Center** (p46) and ogle America's most sky-scraping collection of buildings. In **Millennium Park** (pictured; p34), watch 'the Bean' reflect the skyline and splash under Crown Fountain's human gargoyles.

Explore the masterpieces at the **Art Institute of Chicago** (p38), the nation's second-largest art museum. Next, zip up to the 103rd floor of the **Willis Tower** (p40) and step out onto the glass-floored ledge. (Yes, it's a long way down.)

The West Loop parties in the evening. Sit on the glittery patio sipping some bubbly at **RM Champagne Salon** (p126) or down a cocktail made with the house vodka at **CH Distillery** (p125).

Day 2

FRASER HALL/GETTY IMAGES ©

Stroll up Michigan Ave – aka the **Magnificent Mile** (p60), home of big-name department stores. Wander the half-mile promenade of **Navy Pier** (p56) and take a sky-high spin on the Ferris wheel.

Spend the afternoon at the Museum Campus. Dinosaurs and gemstones stuff the **Field Museum** (p130); sharks swim in the kiddie-mobbed **Shedd Aquarium** (p136). Meteorites and supernovas are on view at the **Adler Planetarium** (p136).

Wander along Wicker Park's Milwaukee Ave and explore booming bars, indie-rock clubs and hipster shops, such as underground bookstore **Quimby's** (p112). Catch live acts at the **Hideout** (p111) or the **Empty Bottle** (p112).

Day 3

D GUEST SMITH/SHUTTERSTOCK ©

Dip your toes in Lake Michigan at **North Avenue Beach** (pictured; p88). Amble northward through the sprawling greenery of **Lincoln Park** (p82). Stop at **Lincoln Park Zoo** (p88) to see lions, zebras and polar bears. Pop into **Lincoln Park Conservatory** (p89) to smell exotic blooms.

Head north to atmospheric, century-old ballpark **Wrigley Field** (p96) for an afternoon baseball game. Afterward practice your home-run swing at **Sluggers** (p100), one of the many rip-roaring bars near the stadium.

Venture to Uptown to Al Capone's favorite, the **Green Mill** (p103) – a timeless venue to hear jazz, watch a poetry slam or swill a martini.

Day 4

JOE HENDRICKSON/SHUTTERSTOCK ©

South in Hyde Park, the **Museum of Science & Industry** (pictured; p142) has acres of exhibits – a German U-boat, mock tornado and exquisite dollhouse for starters. Architecture buffs can tour **Robie House** (p144), Frank Lloyd Wright's Prairie-style masterpiece.

Head back to the Gold Coast for boutique shopping and the **Museum of Contemporary Art** (p70), which always has something provocative showing. Hit the heights of the 94th-floor observatory at **360° Chicago** (p68).

Nightlife options abound in Logan Square. Knock back strong beers at **Revolution Brewing** (p115), then see an arty band for free at wee **Whistler** (p115).

Need to Know
For detailed information, see Survival Guide p147

Currency
US dollar ($)

Language
English

Visas
Generally not required for up to 90 days; check www.travel.state.gov.

Money
ATMs are ubiquitous; credit cards widely accepted.

Cell Phones
International travelers can use local SIM cards in an unlocked smartphone, or buy a cheap US phone with prepaid minutes.

Time
Central Standard Time (GMT/UTC minus six hours)

Tipping
Tipping isn't optional. Waitstaff get 18% to 20%; bartenders $1 to $2 per drink; housekeeping $2 to $5 daily; taxi drivers 10% to 15%.

Daily Budget

Budget: Less than $125
Dorm bed: $35–55
Lunch specials: $10–15
Transit day pass: $10
Discount theater or blues club ticket: $10–25

Midrange: $125–325
Hotel or B&B double room: $175–275
Dinner in a casual restaurant: $25–35
Architecture boat tour: $47
Cubs bleacher seat: $45–65

Top End: More than $325
Luxury hotel double room: $400
Dinner at Alinea: $290
Lyric Opera ticket: $200

Advance Planning

Two months before Book your hotel. Reserve at hot restaurants such as Alinea, Girl & the Goat or Smyth.

Two weeks before Reserve a table at your other must-eat restaurants, and book tickets for sports events and blockbuster museum exhibits.

One week before Check www.hottix.org for half-price theater tickets. Check www.chicagoreader.com to see entertainment options and make bookings.

Arriving in Chicago

✈ O'Hare International Airport

The Blue Line L train ($5) runs 24/7 and departs every 10 minutes or so. To the city center takes 40 minutes. Shuttle vans cost $35, taxis around $50.

✈ Midway International Airport

The Orange Line L train ($3) runs between 4am and 1am, departing every 10 minutes or so. The journey takes 30 minutes to downtown. Shuttle vans cost $28, taxis $35 to $40.

🚆 Union Station

All trains arrive here. The Blue Line Clinton stop is a few blocks south; the Brown, Orange, Purple and Pink Line station at Quincy is a half-mile east. Taxis queue outside the station entrance.

Getting Around

🚆 Train

L trains (pictured) are fast and frequent. Red and Blue Lines operate 24/7, others between roughly 4am and 1am. A day pass is $10.

🚌 Bus

Cover areas that the L misses. Most run from early morning until 10pm; some go later. Some don't run on weekends.

🚕 Taxi

Easy to find downtown, north to Andersonville and west to Wicker Park/Bucktown. Costly.

⚓ Boat

Water taxis travel along the river and lakefront.

🚲 Bicycle

Use abundant rental shops or the Divvy bike-share program.

Chicago Neighborhoods

Lake View & Wrigleyville (p95)
Baseball lovers and nightlife fans share the bar-filled neighborhood, which parties hard, especially in clubthumping Boystown.

Wrigley Field
👁

Lincoln Park & Old Town (p81)
Beaches and zoo animals, top eateries and stylish shops abound in Lincoln Park, while Old Town has Second City comedy.

Wicker Park, Bucktown & Ukranian Village (p105)
Few sights, but you can easily spend the day here shopping and the night eating, drinking and hitting the myriad rock clubs.

West Loop & Near West Side (p117)
Buzzy, top-chef restaurants and trendy bars are the Near West Side's calling card, plus Greek and Italian ethnic enclaves and dynamic art galleries.

Gold Coast (p67)
Furs and Rolls Royces are de rigueur, as are swanky boutiques and cocktail lounges.

Near North & Navy Pier (p55)
Shops, restaurants, hotels, galleries, boats and amusements abound in this densely packed quarter.

The Loop (p33)
Chicago's center of action for both business and play, with skyscrapers galore.

Pilsen & Near South Side (p129)
The lakefront Museum Campus offers a bevy of engaging sights while Chinatown bustles nearby. Mexican taquerias meet hipster hangouts in Pilsen.

Lincoln Park

360° Chicago

Museum of Contemporary Art

Navy Pier

Millennium Park

Art Institute of Chicago

Field Museum of Natural History

Explore
Chicago

Museum of Science & Industry in Jackson Park (p143) JMBATT/GETTY IMAGES ©

Explore ⊕
The Loop

The Loop is Chicago's center of action, named for the elevated train tracks that encircle its busy streets. The Art Institute, Willis Tower, the Theater District and Millennium Park are the top draws among the skyscrapers, while the city's biggest festivals keep people flocking to the area's large green spaces.

The Short List

○ **Millennium Park (p34)** Exploring the freebies of this art-dotted park all day long, from morning yoga classes to afternoon splashes in Crown Fountain and evening concerts at Frank Gehry's band shell.

○ **Art Institute of Chicago (p38)** Admiring color-swirled Monets, Renoirs and one very large Seurat, plus unexpected delights such as the miniature rooms.

○ **Chicago Architecture Center (p46)** Gaping at sky-high ingenuity through an architecture tour by boat or on foot.

○ **Willis Tower (p40)** Stepping onto the glass-floored ledge and peering a loonnngggg way down.

○ **Chicago Cultural Center (p47)** Popping in to see free art exhibitions, concerts and the world's largest Tiffany glass dome.

Getting There & Around

Ⓜ All lines converge in the Loop. Clark/Lake is a useful transfer station between them. Washington/Wabash is handy for the parks, Quincy station for Willis Tower.

🚗 City meters cost $6.50 per hour. Parking lots cost around $40 per day; Millennium Park Garage is one of the cheapest.

Neighborhood Map on p44

L trains running through the Loop CITTADINODELMONDO/GETTY IMAGES ©

Top Sight 📷
Millennium Park

Chicago's showpiece shines with whimsical public art. Where to start amid the mod designs? Perhaps Pritzker Pavilion, Frank Gehry's swooping silver band shell. Jaume Plensa's Crown Fountain, *with its human gargoyles. Anish Kapoor's silvery sculpture* Cloud Gate *(aka 'the Bean'). Or maybe someplace away from the crowds, like the veiled Lurie Garden, abloom with prairie flowers.*

◉ MAP P44, F3

☎ 312-742-1168

www.millenniumpark.org

201 E Randolph St

🕐 6am–11pm

♿

Ⓜ Brown, Orange, Green, Purple, Pink Line to Washington/Wabash

Magic Bean

The park's biggest draw is 'the Bean' – officially titled *Cloud Gate* – Anish Kapoor's 110-ton, silver-drop sculpture. It reflects both the sky and the skyline, and everyone clamors around to take a picture and to touch its silvery smoothness. Good vantage points for photos are at the sculpture's northern and southern ends. For great people-watching, go up the stairs on Washington St, on the Park Grill's northern side, where there are shaded benches.

Crown Fountain

Jaume Plensa's *Crown Fountain* (pictured; p36) is another crowd-pleaser. Its two 50ft-high glass-block towers contain video displays that flash a thousand different faces. The people shown are all native Chicagoans and they all agreed to strap into Plensa's special dental chair, where he immobilized their heads for filming. Each mug puckers up and spurts water, just like the gargoyles atop Notre Dame Cathedral. A fresh set of non-puckering faces appears in winter, when the fountain is dry. On hot days the fountain crowds with locals splashing in the streams to cool off. Kids especially love it.

Pritzker Pavilion

Millennium Park's acoustically awesome band shell Pritzker Pavilion was designed by architect Frank Gehry, who gave it his trademark swooping silver exterior. The pavilion hosts free concerts at 6:30pm several nights weekly from June to August, ranging from indie rock and world music to jazz and classical. On Tuesdays there's usually a movie beamed onto the huge screen on stage. Seats are available up close in the pavilion, or you can sit on the grassy Great Lawn that unfurls behind.

For all shows – but especially the classical ones, which the top-notch Grant Park Orchestra performs – folks bring blankets, picnics,

★ Top Tips

o The Family Fun Tent in the park's northwest corner offers free crafts and games for kids between 10am and 2pm daily in summer.

o Concessions and bathrooms are available by the outdoor cafe/ice rink on Michigan Ave.

o Free walking tours of the park (at 11:30am and 1pm daily from late May to mid-October) leave from the Chicago Cultural Center's Randolph St lobby.

✗ Take a Break

Grab a burger and creamy-thick milkshake at the **Shake Shack** (☏312-646-6005; www.shakeshack.com; 12 S Michigan Ave; burgers $5-10; ☉11am-11pm) on Michigan Ave.

Go French with a baguette and café au lait at Toni Patisserie & Cafe (p52).

wine and beer. There is nothing quite like sitting on the lawn, looking up through Gehry's wild grid and seeing the grandeur of the skyscrapers forming the backdrop to the soaring music. If you want a seat up close, arrive early. Find more information at www.grantpark musicfestival.com.

Lurie Garden

If the crowds at the Bean, *Crown Fountain* and Pritzker Pavilion are too much, seek out the peaceful **Lurie Garden** (www.luriegarden. org; ⊕6am-11pm; Ⓜ Brown, Orange, Green, Purple, Pink Line to Randolph), which uses native plants to form a botanical tribute to Illinois' tallgrass prairie. Visitors often miss the area as it's hidden behind a big hedge. Yellow coneflowers, poet's daffodils,

bluebells and other gorgeous blooms carpet the 5-acre oasis; everything is raised sustainably and without chemicals. A little river runs through it, where folks kick off their shoes and dangle their feet.

From mid-May to mid-September, volunteers lead free tours through the garden on Thursday and Friday between 11am and 1:15pm, and on Sunday between 11am and 2:15pm. They last around 20 minutes and depart every 15 to 20 minutes. No reservations are required; just show up at the southern end of the boardwalk.

BP Bridge & Nichols Bridgeway

In addition to Pritzker Pavilion, architect Frank Gehry also designed the snaking BP Bridge (pictured; p34)

James Plensa's *Crown Fountain* (p35)

that spans Columbus Dr. The luminous sheet-metal walkway connects Millennium Park (from the back of the Great Lawn) to the new Maggie Daley Park (p46), which has ice-skating and rock climbing among its activity arsenal. The bridge offers great skyline views too.

The Nichols Bridgeway is another pedestrian-only span. Renzo Piano designed this silver beauty. It arches from the park over Monroe St to the Art Institute's 3rd-floor contemporary sculpture terrace (which is free to view). Piano, incidentally, also designed the museum's Modern Wing, which is where the sculpture terrace is located.

Cycling & Ice-Skating

The McDonald's Cycle Center, in the park's northeastern corner near the intersection of Randolph St and Columbus Dr, is the city's main facility for bike commuters, with 300 bike-storage spaces plus showers. It's also a convenient place to pick up rental bikes from Bike & Roll (p150), including road, hybrid, tandem and children's bikes.

Tucked between the Bean sculpture and the twinkling lights of Michigan Ave, the McCormick Tribune Ice Rink fills with skaters in winter. It operates from late November to late February and it is hands down the city's

Park History

Millennium Park was originally slated to open in 2000 to coincide with the millennium (hence the name), but construction delays and escalating costs pushed it back. The whole thing seemed headed for disaster, since the original budget was $150 million but costs were rising far in excess of that. The final bill came to $475 million. Private donors ended up paying $200 million to complete the project.

most scenic rink. Admission is free; skate rental costs $13 to $15 (more on weekends). Free lessons start an hour before the rink opens. In summer the rink morphs into the alfresco cafe of the Park Grill.

Wrigley Square & Boeing Galleries

The big plaza at the corner of Michigan Ave and Randolph St is Wrigley Square. The Greek-looking structure rising up from it is the **Millennium Monument**, a replica of the original peristyle that stood here between 1917 and 1953. The semicircular row of Doric columns shoots up nearly 40ft. It juxtaposes oddly with the modern art throughout the rest of the park, but it's meant to tie past and present together. The lawn in front is dandy for lazing about.

Top Sight 📷
Art Institute of Chicago

The USA's second-largest art museum, the Art Institute houses a treasure trove from around the globe. The collection of impressionist and postimpressionist paintings is second only to those in France, and the number of surrealist works is tremendous. The Modern Wing dazzles with Picassos and Mirós, while Japanese prints, Grecian urns and suits of armor stuff endless rooms beyond.

◉ MAP P44, E4

✆ 312-443-3600

www.artic.edu

111 S Michigan Ave

adult/child $25/free

🕐 10:30am-5pm Fri-Wed, to 8pm Thu

Ⓜ Brown, Orange, Green, Purple, Pink Line to Adams

Must-See Works: Floor 2

Get close enough to Georges Seurat's *A Sunday Afternoon on the Island of La Grande Jatte* (Gallery 240) to view its component dots and you'll see why it took the artist two years to complete his pointillist masterpiece. *The Bedroom* (Gallery 241) by Vincent van Gogh depicts the sleeping quarters of the artist's house in Arles. Claude Monet's *Stacks of Wheat* (Gallery 243) – paintings of the 15ft-tall stacks by the artist's farmhouse in Giverny – were part of a series that effectively launched his career in 1891. *Nighthawks* (Gallery 262), Edward Hopper's poignant snapshot of four solitary souls at a neon-lit diner, was inspired by a Manhattan restaurant. Grant Wood used his sister and his dentist as models for the stern-faced farmers in his iconic *American Gothic* (Gallery 263).

Must-See Works: Floors 1 & 3

Marc Chagall created the huge, blue stained-glass *America Windows* (Gallery 144) to celebrate the USA's bicentennial. The elongated figure of *The Old Guitarist* (Gallery 391) by Pablo Picasso is from the artist's Blue Period, reflecting not only a color scheme but Picasso's early experience as a poor artist in Paris. Salvador Dalí's *Inventions of the Monsters* (Gallery 396) was painted in Austria immediately before the Nazi annexation. The title refers to a Nostradamus prediction that the apparition of monsters presages the outbreak of war.

Other Intriguing Sights

The Thorne Miniature Rooms (Lower Level, Gallery 11) and Paperweight Collection (Lower Level, Gallery 15) are awesome, overlooked galleries. In the light-drenched Modern Wing, the ongoing exhibition *The New Contemporary* (Galleries 288 and 290–99) bursts with iconic works by Andy Warhol, Roy Lichtenstein and Jasper Johns.

★ Top Tips

○ Allow two hours to browse the museum's highlights; art buffs should allocate much longer.

○ Advance tickets are available online (surcharge $2), but unless there's a blockbuster exhibit on they're usually not necessary.

○ Ask at the information desk about free talks and tours once you're inside.

○ Download the museum's free app using the on-site wi-fi. It offers several audio tours through the collection.

✗ Take a Break

The Gage (p50) cooks eclectic gastropub fare and pours whiskeys and beers to pair with it.

The Berghoff (p50), dating from 1898, is tops for a beer and a dose of Chicago history.

Top Sight 📷
Willis Tower

For superlative-seekers, Willis Tower is it: Chicago's tallest skyscraper, rising 1450ft into the heavens. Built in 1973 as the Sears Tower, the black-tubed behemoth reigned as the world's tallest building for almost 25 years. It still wins the prize for views from its 103rd-floor Skydeck, where glass-floored ledges jut out in midair and give a knee-buckling perspective straight down.

◎ MAP P44, B4

☏ 312-875-9696

www.theskydeck.com

233 S Wacker Dr

adult/child $24/16

🕘 9am-10pm Mar-Sep, 10am-8pm Oct-Feb, last entry 30 min prior

Ⓜ Brown, Orange, Purple, Pink Line to Quincy

Facts & Stats

Before ascending, there are factoid-filled murals to ponder and an informational movie to watch. You'll learn about the 43,000 miles of phone cable used, the 2232 steps to the roof, and how the tower height is the equivalent of 313 Oprahs (or 262 Michael Jordans). Then it's time for the ear-popping, 70-second elevator ride to the top. From here, the entire city stretches below and you can see exactly how Chicago is laid out. On good days you can see for 40 to 50 miles, as far as Indiana, Michigan and Wisconsin. (On hazy or stormy days you won't see much at all, so don't bother.)

Architecture

Fazlur Khan came up with the design of nine bundled tubes after looking at cigarettes in their pack. The structure lost its 'world's tallest' crown in 1996 to Malaysia's Petronas Twin Towers. It lost its 'USA's tallest' crown in 2013 to New York's One World Trade Center.

Ledges

The four ledges are on the deck's western side. They're like glass-encased boxes hanging out from the building's frame. If crowds are light, you can sprawl out on one for the ultimate photo op. The glass is 1.5in thick, so you won't fall. Really. So don't even worry about it.

New Thrills

A new company recently bought the Willis Tower and announced plans to expand the Skydeck's features, though these have yet to be solidified. Soon you might be able to rappel between the 103rd and 102nd floors inside a glass-enclosed box, or take a 'ledge walk' on a glass-pane balcony. Keep an eye on the sky here for more on the unnerving possibilities to come.

★ Top Tips

o Avoid peak times in summer, between 11am and 4pm Friday to Sunday, when queues can surpass an hour.

o Buying tickets online saves some time, but there's a $2 surcharge per ticket.

o The entrance is on Jackson Blvd, where you go through security. The line to pay is down one level (staff will direct you there).

o Ask at the entrance and/or ticket desk about visibility. Staff can call the Skydeck and provide updates.

✗ Take a Break

Choose from some of Chicago's best fast-casual dining brands and wash it down with a cocktail at Revival Food Hall (p49).

Global vegan dishes and organic wines feature at Native Foods Cafe (p49).

Walking Tour 🥾

The Loop's
Art & Architecture

Why buy postcards when you can make your own? With a camera and some comfortable shoes you can have your own picture-postcard perspective of this charmingly photogenic city. This tour winds through the Loop and across the Chicago River, passing some of the city's finest old buildings and notable public art.

Walk Facts

Start Chicago Board of Trade (Ⓜ Brown, Orange, Purple, Pink Line to La Salle)

End Tribune Tower (Ⓜ Red Line to Grand)

Length 3 miles; about two hours

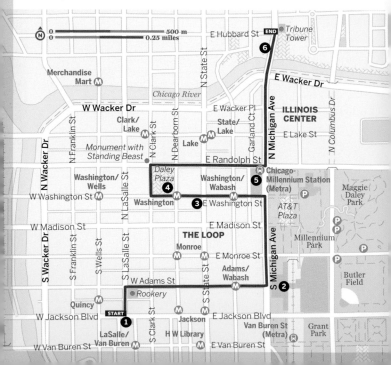

❶ Chicago Board of Trade & Rookery

Start at the **Chicago Board of Trade** (141 W Jackson Blvd;), a 1930 art deco temple of commerce. It was established in 1848 to trade wheat and other farm produce, hence the statue of Ceres, the Roman goddess of agriculture, atop the building. The nearby **Rookery** (📞312-994-4000; www.flwright. org; 209 S LaSalle St; 🕘9am-5pm Mon-Fri) features the work of two famed Chicago architects. Built in 1888 by Daniel Burnham, the monumental brick building maximized light and air with a central atrium; Frank Lloyd Wright redesigned the lobby 19 years later.

❷ Art Institute of Chicago & Millennium Park

Head east on Adams to the **Art Institute** (p38), one of the world's finest art museums; the bronze lions out front offer perfect selfie spots. Just north is **Millennium Park** (p34), filled with avant-garde works from world-famous names such as Frank Gehry and Anish Kapoor.

❸ Reliance Building

Two blocks west on Washington is the 1895 **Reliance Building** (1 W Washington St), another Burnham design; its white terra-cotta facade and large windows were groundbreaking. A posh hotel today, it originally housed medi-cal offices – Al Capone's dentist practiced in room 809.

❹ Picasso & Dubuffet

Another block west is Pablo Picasso's **untitled sculpture** (50 W Washington St). He never revealed what it portrayed – popular guesses include a woman, a dog or a baboon – so interpret it however you like. Just northwest is another inscrutable sculpture, Jean Dubuffet's **Monument with Standing Beast** (100 W Randolph St).

❺ Chicago Cultural Center

Walk east on Randolph to beaux-arts beauty the **Chicago Cultural Center** (p47). Pop inside to see the world's largest Tiffany stained-glass dome (and perhaps even a free concert).

❻ Wrigley Building & Tribune Tower

Continue north over the Chicago River to finish up at two of Chicago's most famous edifices: the gleaming-white terra-cotta **Wrigley Building** (p61) and the neo-Gothic **Tribune Tower** (p60), whose base contains fragments from notable international constructions (the Berlin Wall, the Taj Mahal). From here you can continue to explore Chicago's Near North and Navy Pier.

The Loop

1

Merchandise Mart Ⓜ

Chicago Water Taxi, LaSalle St

Chicago River

W Wacker Dr

333 W Wacker Dr

W Lake St

19 🍴 Clark/Lake Ⓜ Lake State/Lake Ⓜ

24 ⭐

2

N Canal St N Wacker Dr N Franklin St N Wells St N LaSalle St N Clark St N Dearborn St N State St

W Randolph St

County Building & Chicago City Hall

Richard J Daley Center

Washington/ Wells Ⓜ

Daley Plaza

Washington Ⓜ

W Washington St Ⓜ

Chicago Water Taxi, Ogilvie/Union 🚉

25 ⭐

W Calhoun Pl

THE LOOP

E Calhoun Pl

3

South Branch Chicago River

S Canal St S Wacker Dr

W Madison St

Chase Building

● Target

W Monroe St

Monroe Ⓜ

S Franklin St S Wells St S LaSalle St S Clark St S State St

W Marble Pl

11 ❌

4

Shoreline Water Taxi, Willis Tower/Union Station

W Adams St

Quincy Ⓜ W Quincy St

13 ❌

Post Office

Chicago Federal Center

17 🚉

🚉 Chicago-Union Station (Metra)

Willis Tower

3 ◎ *Money Museum*

W Jackson Blvd

6 ◎ Jackson Ⓜ

Kluczynski Federal Building

Chicago Board of Trade

S Financial Pl

5

W Van Buren St

LaSalle/ Van Buren Ⓜ

S Federal St S Dearborn St

H W Library

Harold Washington Library Center

LaSalle Ⓜ

W Congress Pkwy

🚉 Chicago-LaSalle St Station (Metra)

14 ❌

6

W Harrison St

Harrison Ⓜ

S Wells St S Financial Pl S LaSalle St S Clark St S State St

A B C D

Sights

Chicago Architecture Center
GALLERY

1 ◉ MAP P44, E1

The CAC is the premier keeper of Chicago's architectural flame. Pop in to explore its excellent galleries, which feature an interactive 3-D model of Chicago and displays on the city's architectural history, as well as giant models of and exhibits on skyscrapers around the world and the amazing technologies needed to build them, from construction to security to sustainability. You can also check out the CAC's extensive roster of boat and walking tours (p20) and make bookings here. (CAC; ☎312-922-3432; www.architecture.org; 111 E Wacker Dr; adult/student/child $12/8/free; ⏱9:30am-5pm; 🚌151, Ⓜ Brown, Orange, Green, Purple, Pink Line to Clark/Lake)

Aqua Tower
ARCHITECTURE

2 ◉ MAP P44, F1

Aqua made waves when it appeared in 2009. Local architect Jeanne Gang designed the 86-story tower (set to be surpassed in 2020, when her 93-story Vista Tower will open nearby). Dramatic undulating balconies curve out from the core, interspersed with reflective glass that forms 'pools' shimmering from the white rippled tiers. The Radisson Blu Aqua Hotel takes up floors 1 to 18; the remaining floors hold multi million-dollar apartments and offices. (225 N Columbus Dr; Ⓜ Brown, Orange, Green, Purple, Pink Line to State/Lake)

Money Museum
MUSEUM

3 ◉ MAP P44, C4

This small museum in the Federal Reserve Bank of Chicago is fun for a quick browse. The best exhibits include a giant glass cube stuffed with one million $1 bills (they weigh 2000lb) and a counterfeit display differentiating real bills from fakes. Learn why we call $1000 a 'grand'; learn more about Alexander Hamilton and his creation of a new nation's financial infrastructure; and snap a sweet photo clutching the million-dollar-stuffed briefcase. (☎312-322-2400; www.chicagofed.org; 230 S LaSalle St; admission free; ⏱8:30am-5pm Mon-Fri; Ⓜ Brown, Orange, Purple, Pink Line to Quincy)

Maggie Daley Park
PARK

4 ◉ MAP P44, G3

Families love this park's fanciful, free playgrounds in all their enchanted-forest and pirate-themed glory. There's also a rock-climbing wall, an 18-hole mini-golf course, a winding, in-line skating track called the Skating Ribbon (used for ice-skating in winter) and tennis courts; these features have various fees. Multiple picnic tables make the park an excellent spot to relax. The pedestrian BP Bridge (p36) connects it to the Millennium Park. (www.maggiedaleypark.com; 337 E Randolph St; ⏱6am-11pm;

🚻; Ⓜ Brown, Orange, Green, Purple, Pink Line to Washington/Wabash)

Chicago Cultural Center
NOTABLE BUILDING

5 ◉ MAP P44, E2

This exquisite, beaux-arts building began its life as the Chicago Public Library in 1897. Today the block-long structure houses terrific art exhibitions (especially the 4th-floor Yates Gallery), as well as classical concerts at lunchtime every Wednesday (12:15pm). It also contains the world's largest Tiffany stained-glass dome, on the 3rd floor where the library circulation desk used to be. InstaGreeter (p20) tours of the Loop depart from the Randolph St lobby, as do Millennium Park tours. And it's all free! (📞312-744-6630; www.chicagoculturalcenter.org; 78 E Washington St; admission free; ⏱10am-7pm Mon-Fri, to 5pm Sat & Sun; Ⓜ Brown, Orange, Green, Purple, Pink Line to Washington/Wabash)

Kluczynski Federal Building
ARCHITECTURE

6 ◉ MAP P44, D4

No discussion of famed Loop architecture is complete without mentioning the boxy, metal-and-glass style of Ludwig Mies van der Rohe, whose functional, stripped-bare design became the standard for modern skyscrapers. The 1974 Kluczynski Building, part of the **Chicago Federal Center**, is a prime example. It demonstrates both the geometric, open spaces

Tiffany glass ceiling, Chicago Cultural Center

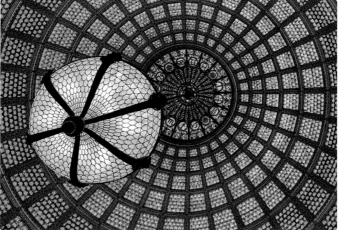

and starkly minimalist vertical I-beams he favored. (230 S Dearborn St; **M** Blue Line to Jackson)

Buckingham Fountain FOUNTAIN

7 ⊙ MAP P44, G5

Grant Park's centerpiece is one of the world's largest fountains, with a 1.5-million-gallon capacity and a 15-story-high spray. It lets loose on the hour from 9am to 11pm early May to mid-October, accompanied at night by multicolored lights and music. (301 S Columbus Dr; **M** Red Line to Harrison)

Route 66 Sign HISTORIC SITE

8 ⊙ MAP P44, E4

Attention Route 66 buffs: the Mother Road begins in downtown Chicago. Look for the 'Historic 66 Begin' sign at the northwestern corner of Adams St and Michigan Ave, across from the Art Institute. (There's another sign at the end of the block, but this one is a replica of the original.) From Chicago the route traverses 2400 miles to Los Angeles, past neon signs, mom-and-pop motels and pie-and-coffee diners...but it all starts here. (E Adams St, btwn S Michigan & Wabash Aves; **M** Brown, Orange, Green, Purple, Pink Line to Adams)

American Writers Museum MUSEUM

9 ⊙ MAP P44, E2

Bibliophiles will have a grand time in this museum, where American

writers spanning the ages – from Edgar Allan Poe to Elie Wiesel, James Baldwin to Edith Wharton – get their due. Interactive exhibits trace the history of the American voice in nonfiction and literature, while rotating displays celebrate individual wordsmiths. Another exhibit provides exercises and tips for your own writing (along with a table of old typewriters). The colorful Children's Literature gallery features story times and books to read. (www.americanwritersmuseum.org; 180 N Michigan Ave, 2nd fl; adult/child $12/free; ⊙10am-5pm; 🚻; **M** Brown, Orange, Green, Purple, Pink Line to Randolph or State/Lake)

Riverwalk WATERFRONT

10 ⊙ MAP P44, E1

Winding along the Chicago River's southern side next to Wacker Dr, this 1.25-mile-long promenade is a fine spot to escape the crowds and watch boats glide by. Access it from the stairs at any bridge. Outdoor cafes, umbrella-shaded bars, a kayak-rental shop and a fountain you can splash in dot the way. The broad steps between Clark and LaSalle Sts offer a good refuge to sit and relax. (www.chicagoriverwalk.us; Chicago River waterfront, btwn N Lake Shore Dr & W Lake St; ⊙6am-11pm; **M** Brown, Orange, Green, Purple, Pink, Blue Line to State/Lake)

Eating

Revival Food Hall   AMERICAN $

11 ⊗ MAP P44, C4

The Loop needed a forward-thinking food court, and Revival Food Hall delivered. Come lunchtime, hip office workers pack the blond-wood tables of this ground-floor modern marketplace in the historic National building. The all-local dining concept brings 15 of Chicago's best fast-casual food outlets to the masses, from Antique Taco and Smoque BBQ to Furious Spoon ramen and HotChocolate Bakery. (☎773-999-9411; www.revivalfoodhall.com; 125 S Clark St; mains $7-12; ⊕7am-7pm Mon-Fri; ☎; Ⓜ Blue Line to Monroe)

Pastoral   DELI $

12 ⊗ MAP P44, E2

Pastoral makes a mean sandwich. Fresh-shaved serrano ham, Calabrese salami and other carnivorous fixings meet smoky mozzarella, Gruyère and piquant spreads slathered on crusty baguettes. Vegetarians also have options. There's limited seating; most folks take away for picnics in Millennium Park (call in your order a few hours in advance to avoid a queue). (☎312-658-1250; www.pastoralartisan.com; 53 E Lake St; sandwiches $8-11; ⊕10:30am-8pm Mon-Fri, 11am-6pm Sat & Sun; ☝; Ⓜ Brown, Orange, Green, Purple, Pink Line to Randolph or State/Lake)

Daley Plaza   🍽

Picasso's eye-popping untitled sculpture marks the heart of **Daley Plaza** (Map p44, C2), which is the place to be come lunchtime, particularly when the weather warms up. You never know what will be going on – dance performances, bands, ethnic festivals, holiday celebrations – but you do know it'll be free. A summertime farmers market sets up on Thursday (7am to 3pm, May to October) and food trucks add to the action once a week (11am to 3pm, often on Friday) from March through October.

Native Foods Cafe   VEGAN $

13 ⊗ MAP P44, C4

For tasty, vegan fast-casual fare, Native Foods is your spot. The big ol' BBQ burger features seitan bacon and melted mock American cheese on a plant-based patty; try it with the signature nacho fries. Local beers and organic wines accompany the wide-ranging, internationally inspired menu, which features changing seasonal dishes. Soy-free, gluten-free and nut-free allergy menus are available. (☎312-332-6332; www.nativefoods.com; 218 S Clark St; mains $9-12; ⊕10:30am-9pm Mon-Sat, 11am-7pm Sun; ☝; Ⓜ Brown, Orange, Purple, Pink Line to Quincy)

Epic Burger

BURGERS $

14 MAP P44, D6

This sprawling, sunny-orange restaurant beloved by South Loop college students brings eco-conscious fast-food eaters the goods they crave: burgers made with all-natural beef, no hormones or antibiotics, topped with cage-free organic eggs and nitrate-free bacon; preservative-free buns; vanilla-bean-speckled milkshakes; and no petroleum-based packaging. Some vegan options, too. No cash accepted – credit cards only. (312-913-1373; www.epicburger.com; 517 S State St; mains $4-8; 10:30am-10pm Mon-Thu, to 11pm Fri & Sat, to 9pm Sun; ; MBrown, Orange, Purple, Pink Line to Library)

Pizano's

PIZZA $$

15 MAP P44, E3

Pizano's is a good recommendation for deep-dish newbies, since it's not jaw-breakingly thick. The thin-crust pies that hit the checker-clothed tables are good too, winning rave reviews for crispness. Some of the waitstaff are characters who've been around forever, which adds to the convivial ambience. It's open late-night (with a full bar), which is a Loop rarity. (312-236-1777; www.pizanoschicago.com; 61 E Madison St; small pizzas from $16; 11am-2am Sun-Fri, to 3am Sat; ; MRed, Blue Line to Monroe)

Gage

GASTROPUB $$$

16 MAP P44, E3

This always-hopping gastropub dishes up fanciful grub, from Gouda-topped venison burgers to mussels vindaloo or Guinness-battered fish and chips; a steak menu offers massive cuts. The booze rocks too, including a solid whiskey list and small-batch beers that pair with the food. (312-372-4243; www.thegagechicago.com; 24 S Michigan Ave; mains $15-36, steaks $47-65; 11am-11pm Mon-Thu, to midnight Fri, 10am-midnight Sat, 10am-10pm Sun; MBrown, Orange, Green, Purple, Pink Line to Washington/Wabash)

Drinking

Berghoff

BAR

17 MAP P44, D4

The Berghoff dates from 1898 and was the first Chicago bar to serve a legal drink after Prohibition (ask to see the liquor license stamped '#1'). Little has changed around the antique wood bar since. Belly up for mugs of local and imported beers and order sauerbraten, schnitzel and pretzels the size of

---

Musical Picnics

Gather the makings of a picnic meal and meander over to Millennium Park to hear a free concert. Indie rock, jazz or classical performers take the stage nightly in summer, including many big-name musicians. Pastoral (p49) and Toni Patisserie can set you up with deli goods and wine.

your head from the adjoining German restaurant. (📞312-427-3170; www.theberghoff.com; 17 W Adams St; 🕐11am-9pm Mon-Fri, from 11:30am Sat; Ⓜ️Blue, Red Line to Jackson)

Cindy's

BAR

19 Ⓠ MAP P44, E3

Cindy's unfurls awesome views of Millennium Park and the lake from atop the Chicago Athletic Association Hotel. Sit at one of the long wood tables under twinkling lights and sip snazzy cocktails with ingredients such as orange saffron bitters. Alas, everyone wants in on the action, so come early to avoid having to wait for a seat. (📞312-792-3502; www.cindysrooftop.com; 12 S Michigan Ave; 🕐11am-1am Mon-Fri, 10am-2am Sat, 10am-midnight Sun;

Ⓜ️Brown, Orange, Green, Purple, Pink Line to Washington/Wabash)

Monk's Pub

PUB

19 Ⓠ MAP P44, B2

Pull open the huge wooden doors and enter this dimly lit Belgian beer cave. Old barrels, vintage taps and faux antiquarian books set the mood, accompanied by a whopping international brew selection (almost 200!) and free peanuts. Office workers and the occasional TV weather presenter are the main folks hanging out at Monk's, which also serves good, burgery pub grub. (📞312-357-6665; www.monkspubchicago.com; 205 W Lake St; 🕐9am-11pm Mon-Wed, to 2am Thu & Fri, 11am-5pm Sat; 📶; Ⓜ️Blue, Brown, Orange, Green, Purple, Pink Line to Clark/Lake)

The Berghoff

Toni Patisserie & Cafe CAFE

20 🚇 MAP P44, E3

Toni's provides a cute refuge for a glass of wine. The Parisian-style cafe has a small list of French red, white and sparkling wines to sip at close-set tables while you try to resist the éclairs, macarons and tiered cakes tempting you from the glass case. It also sells bottles for takeout – handy for park picnics. (☎312-726-2020; www.tonipatisserie.com; 65 E Washington St; ⏱7am-7pm Mon-Fri, from 8am Sat, 9am-5pm Sun; Ⓜ Brown, Orange, Green, Purple, Pink Line to Washington/Wabash)

Summer Dance

To boogie with a multi-ethnic mash-up of locals, head to the Spirit of Music Garden in Grant Park for **Summer Dance** (Map p44; E6; www.chicagosummerdance.org; 601 S Michigan Ave; ⏱6-9pm Wed, to 9:30pm Thu-Sat, 4-7pm Sun late Jun-Aug; Ⓜ Red Line to Harrison). Bands play a wide range of toe-stepping music: swing, house, rumba, samba, Afrobeat and other styles, preceded by an hour of fun dance lessons – all free. Ballroom-quality moves are absolutely not required.

Entertainment

Grant Park Orchestra CLASSICAL MUSIC

21 ⭐ MAP P44, F2

It's a summertime must-do. The Grant Park Orchestra – composed of top-notch musicians from symphonies worldwide – puts on free classical concerts at Millennium Park's Pritzker Pavilion (p35). Patrons bring lawn chairs, blankets, wine and picnic fixings to set the scene as the sun dips, the skyscraper lights flicker on and glorious music fills the night air. (☎312-742-7638; www.grantparkmusicfestival.com; Pritzker Pavilion, Millennium Park; ⏱6:30pm Wed & Fri, 7:30pm Sat mid-Jun–mid-Aug; Ⓜ Brown, Orange, Green, Purple, Pink Line to Washington/Wabash)

Buddy Guy's Legends BLUES

22 ⭐ MAP P44, E6

Top local and national acts wail on the stage of local icon Buddy Guy. The man himself usually plays a series of shows in January; tickets go on sale in October. Free, all-ages acoustic shows are staged at lunch and dinner (the place doubles as a Cajun restaurant); note that you must pay to stay on for late-evening shows. (☎312-427-1190; www.buddyguy.com; 700 S Wabash Ave; cover charge Sun-Thu $10, Fri & Sat $20; ⏱5pm-2am Mon & Tue, from 11am Wed-Fri, noon-3am Sat, noon-2am Sun; Ⓜ Red Line to Harrison)

Chicago Symphony Orchestra
CLASSICAL MUSIC

23 ⭐ MAP P44, E4

Riccardo Muti leads the CSO, one of America's best symphonies, known for its fervent subscribers and an untouchable brass section. Cellist Yo-Yo Ma is the creative consultant and a frequent soloist. The season runs from September to June at Symphony Center; Daniel Burnham designed the Orchestra Hall. (CSO; 312-294-3000; www.cso.org; 220 S Michigan Ave; M Brown, Orange, Green, Purple, Pink Line to Adams)

Goodman Theatre
THEATER

24 ⭐ MAP P44, D2

One of Chicago's premier drama houses, with a gorgeous Theater District facility. It specializes in new and classic American productions and has been cited several times as one of the USA's best regional theaters. Unsold tickets for the current day's performance go on sale at 10am for half-price online; they're also available at the box office from noon. (312-443-3800; www.goodmantheatre.org; 170 N Dearborn St; M Brown, Orange, Green, Purple, Pink, Blue Line to Clark/Lake)

Lyric Opera of Chicago
OPERA

25 ⭐ MAP P44, A3

Tickets are hard to come by for this bold modern opera company, which fills the chandeliered Civic Opera House with a shrewd mix of common classics and daring premieres from September to May. If your Italian isn't up to snuff, don't worry – the company projects English 'supertitles' above the proscenium. (312-827-5600; www.lyricopera.org; 20 N Wacker Dr; M Brown, Orange, Purple, Pink Line to Washington/Wells)

Shopping

Chicago Architecture Center Shop
GIFTS & SOUVENIRS

Browse through skyline T-shirts and posters, Frank Lloyd Wright note cards, skyscraper models and heaps of books that celebrate local architecture at this haven for anyone with an edifice complex; a children's section has books to pique the interest of budding builders. The items make excellent 'only in Chicago' souvenirs. Located in the Chicago Architecture Center (see 1 ◉ Map p44, E1). (312-922-3432; www.shop.architecture.org; 111 E Wacker Dr; ◷ 9am-5pm Mon, Wed & Fri-Sun, to 8pm Tue & Thu; ▣ 151, M Brown, Orange, Green, Purple, Pink Line to State/Lake)

ShopColumbia
ART

26 🔒 MAP P44, E6

This is Columbia College's student store, where student artists and designers sell their wares. The shop carries original, handcrafted pieces spanning all media and disciplines: clothes, jewelry, prints, mugs, paintings, stationery and more. Students earn 75% of the price, and part of the proceeds also goes toward student scholarships. (312-369-8616; www.shop.colum.edu; 619 S Wabash Ave; ◷ 11am-5pm Mon-Fri; M Red Line to Harrison)

Explore

Near North & Navy Pier

The Near North packs in deep-dish-pizza parlors, buzzy bistros, art galleries and so many upscale stores that its main vein — Michigan Ave — has been dubbed the 'Magnificent Mile.' Bulging out to the east is Navy Pier, a half-mile-long wharf of tour boats, carnival rides and a flashy, king-sized Ferris wheel.

The Short List

○ **Navy Pier (p56)** Walking on the boat-bedecked wharf and taking in the views — especially from the stomach-churning 196ft Ferris wheel.

○ **Giordano's (p63)** Hefting a gooey slice of pizza that's even mightier than deep-dish.

○ **Magnificent Mile (p60)** Shopping with the frenzied masses along this busy stretch of Michigan Ave jam-packed with retailers from Burberry to Nike to a very spiffy Apple.

○ **Driehaus Museum (p60)** Ogling the gilded mansion's marble stairwells, French porcelain vases, bronze candelabras and Tiffany stained glass.

Getting There & Around

Ⓜ Red Line to Grand or Chicago for the Magnificent Mile; Brown, Purple Line to Chicago or Merchandise Mart for River North.

🚌 A free trolley runs from the Red Line Grand stop to Navy Pier from late May to early September.

🚗 Parking garages (around $35 per day) dominate near the Mag Mile. Metered parking ($4 per hour) becomes more common as you move west.

Neighborhood Map on p58

Navy Pier giant swing (p57) NAEBLYS/SHUTTERSTOCK ©

Top Sight 📷
Navy Pier

Navy Pier was once the city's municipal wharf. Today it's Chicago's most visited attraction, with eight million people per year flooding its half-mile length. Locals may groan about its commercialization, but even they can't refute the brilliant lakefront views, cool breezes and whopping fireworks displays in summer. Kids go gaga over the high-tech rides, fast-food restaurants and trinket vendors.

⊙ MAP P58, H4

📞 312-595-7437

www.navypier.com

600 E Grand Ave; 🚌 65

admission free

🕙 10am-10pm Sun-Thu, to midnight Fri & Sat Jun-Aug, 10am-8pm Sun-Thu, to 10pm Fri & Sat Sep-May

Centennial Wheel & Other Rides

No visit to the pier is complete without a stomach-curdling turn on the gigantic, 196ft-tall **Centennial Wheel** (adult/child $18/15), which unfurls great views. The **carousel** (per ride $9; ⏱May-Oct) is a beloved kiddie classic, with carved horses bobbing to organ music. There's also a **giant swing** that spins you out over the pier. Each attraction costs $9 to $18. For the young ones, the Chicago Children's Museum (p60) is on the pier near the main entrance.

Theaters & Tour Boats

Besides an **IMAX Theater** (☎312-595-5629; www.amctheatres.com; tickets $15-22), the Pier hosts the **Chicago Shakespeare Theater** (☎312-595-5600; www.chicagoshakes.com), which shows populist takes on the Bard in the white-canopied 'tent', a new venue called the Yard. Competing tour boats depart from the pier's southern side, where you can set sail in everything from a tall-masted schooner (p20) to thrill-ride **speedboat** (☎888-636-7737; www.seadogcruises.com; tours $28-35; ⏱Mar-Oct).

Plazas & Events

Polk Bros Park, by the pier's entrance, entertains with a splashy fountain with lights and dancing spouts. Feel free to jump in with all the kids doing the same. Performance lawns feature free concerts and movies. Other spots to relax include the **Wave Wall** stairs overlooking the lake; the **Crystal Gardens**, with palm trees and tables under a soaring glass roof; and the big wood lounge chairs that dot the pier. All of these areas are part of a pier renovation project; last to come is a hotel at the pier's eastern end, due for completion by summer 2020.

★ **Top Tips**

o Crowds amass for the summer fireworks shows on Wednesday at 9:30pm and Saturday at 10:15pm.

o In summer the **Shoreline Water Taxi** (www.shorelinesightseeing.com; adult/child Mon-Thu $8/4, Fri-Sun $10/5) glides from Navy Pier to the Museum Campus.

o Vendors sell beer and alcohol from walk-up windows, so you can stroll and drink on the pier.

✕ **Take a Break**

Heft a slice of stuffed pizza at the pier outpost of **Giordano's** (☎312-288-8783; www.giordanos.com; 700 E Grand Ave, Navy Pier; small pizzas from $18; ⏱10am-9pm Sun-Thu, to 10pm Fri & Sat; 🚌65). Seek out **Original Rainbow Cone**, in a kiosk halfway down the pier on the south side. A scoop is actually five 'slices' of different flavored ice cream.

Sights

Driehaus Museum
MUSEUM

1 ⊙ MAP P58, C3

Set in the exquisite Nickerson Mansion, the Driehaus immerses visitors in Gilded Age decorative arts and architecture. You'll feel like a *Great Gatsby* character as you wander three floors stuffed with sumptuous objets d'art and heaps of Tiffany stained glass. Recommended guided tours ($5 extra) are available four times daily. The price seems steep, but the museum is a prize for those intrigued by opulent interiors. (☏312-482-8933; www.driehausmuseum.org; 40 E Erie St, River North; adult/child $20/free; ⊙10am-5pm Tue-Sun; Ⓜ Red Line to Chicago)

Chicago Children's Museum
MUSEUM

2 ⊙ MAP P58, H4

Designed to challenge the imaginations of toddlers to 10-year-olds, this colorful museum near Navy Pier's main entrance gives young visitors enough hands-on exhibits to keep them climbing and creating for hours. Among the favorites, **Dinosaur Expedition** explores the world of paleontology and lets kids excavate 'bones.' They can also climb a ropey schooner; get wet in **Waterways** (and learn about hydroelectric power); and use real tools to build things in the **Tinkering Lab**. (☏312-527-1000; www.chicagochildrensmuseum.org; 700 E Grand Ave, Navy Pier; $15; ⊙10am-5pm, to 8pm Thu; ♿; ⛴65)

Tribune Tower
ARCHITECTURE

3 ⊙ MAP P58, D4

Take a close look when passing by this 1925 neo-Gothic edifice. Colonel Robert McCormick, eccentric owner of the *Chicago Tribune* in the early 1900s, collected – and asked his reporters to send – rocks from famous buildings and monuments around the world. He stockpiled pieces of the Taj Mahal, Westminster Abbey, the Great Pyramid and more than 140 others, which are now embedded around the tower's base. (435 N Michigan Ave, Streeterville; Ⓜ Red Line to Grand)

Marina City
ARCHITECTURE

4 ⊙ MAP P58, C5

The twin corncob towers of Marina City are an Instagram favorite for their futuristic, cartoony look. Bertrand Goldberg designed the 1964 high-rise, and it has become an iconic part of the Chicago skyline (check out the cover of Wilco's *Yankee Hotel Foxtrot*). And yes, there is a marina at the towers' base. (300 N State St, River North; Ⓜ Brown, Orange, Green, Purple, Pink Line to State/Lake)

Magnificent Mile
AREA

5 ⊙ MAP P58, D3

Spanning N Michigan Ave between the river and Oak St, the 'Mag Mile' is Chicago's much-touted upscale shopping strip, where Bloomingdale's, Apple, Burberry and many more will lighten your wallet. The retailers are mostly high-end chains that have stores nationwide. (www.themagnificent mile.com; N Michigan Ave, Streeterville; M Red Line to Grand)

Wrigley Building ARCHITECTURE

6 💿 MAP P58, D4

The Wrigley Building glows as white as the Doublemint Twins' teeth, day or night. Chewing-gum guy William Wrigley built it that way on purpose, because he wanted it to be attention-grabbing like a billboard. More than 250,000 glazed terra-cotta tiles make up the facade; a computer database tracks each one and indicates when it needs to be cleaned and polished. (400 N Michigan Ave, Streeterville; M Red Line to Grand)

Eating

Billy Goat Tavern BURGERS $

7 ✖ MAP P58, D4

Tribune and *Sun Times* reporters have guzzled in the subterranean Billy Goat for decades. Order a 'cheezborger' and Schlitz beer, then look around at the newspapered walls to get the scoop on infamous local stories, such as the Cubs' Curse. This is a tourist magnet, but a deserving one. Follow the tavern signs leading below Michigan Ave to get here. (📞 312-222-1525; www. billygoattavern.com; 430 N Michigan Ave, lower level, Streeterville; burgers $4-8; 🕑6am-1am Mon-Thu, to 2am Fri, to 3am Sat, 9am-2am Sun; M Red Line to Grand)

Magnificent Mile

Green Door Tavern ¶⊙¶

The **Green Door Tavern** (Map p58, A3; ☎312-664-5496; www.greendoorchicago.com; 678 N Orleans St, River North; mains $10-15; ⏰11:30am-2am Mon-Fri, 10am-3am Sat, 10am-midnight Sun; 🛜; M Brown, Purple Line to Chicago), tucked in an 1872 building, is your place to mingle with locals over a beer and well-made burger amid old photos and memorabilia. During Prohibition, a door painted green meant there was a speakeasy in the basement. It's still there now and now holds a small cocktail bar with jazz singers, burlesque shows, jugglers and other quirky entertainment.

Xoco MEXICAN $

9 ❌ MAP P58, B4

At celeb-chef Rick Bayless' Mexican street-food restaurant (pronounced 'show-co') everything's sourced from local farms. Crunch into warm churros with bean-to-cup hot chocolate for breakfast, and crusty *tortas* (sandwiches, such as the fab mushroom and goat's cheese) and *caldos* (meal-in-a-bowl soups) for lunch and dinner. It's a fast-casual, order-at-the-counter type ambience, where Latin music blares and the metallic decor gleams. (☎312-661-1434;

www.rickbayless.com; 449 N Clark St, River North; mains $9-15; ⏰8am-9pm Tue-Thu, to 10pm Fri & Sat; M Red Line to Grand)

Mr Beef SANDWICHES $

9 ❌ MAP P58, A3

The signature Italian beef sandwich, a Chicago specialty, arrives on a long white bun loaded with thin-cut roast beef that's been simmered and ladled with its own cooking juices. Ask for it 'dipped' (bun and all dunked into the juices) and 'hot' (with *giardiniera*, aka spicy pickled vegetables, added). It's soggy but delicious. Cash only. Don't fear the dumpy decor. (☎312-337-8500; 666 N Orleans St, River North; sandwiches $6-13; ⏰10am-6pm Mon-Thu, to 4am Fri, to 5am Sat; M Brown, Purple Line to Chicago)

Portillo's AMERICAN $

10 ❌ MAP P58, B3

Hot-dog purists might bemoan the lack of true Chicago wieners available in the downtown area, but this outpost of the local Portillo's chain – gussied up with a *nearly* corny 1930s gangster theme – is the place to get one. Try one of its famous dogs and a slice of the heavenly chocolate cake. (☎312-587-8910; www.portillos.com; 100 W Ontario St, River North; mains $4-7; ⏰10am-1am Mon-Sat, to midnight Sun; M Red Line to Grand)

GT Fish & Oyster   SEAFOOD $$

11 ⓧ MAP P58, B4

Seafood restaurants can be fusty. Not so GT Fish & Oyster. The clean-lined room bustles with date-night couples and groups of friends drinking fizzy wines and slurping mollusks. Many of the dishes are shareable, which adds to the convivial, plate-clattering ambience. The sublime clam chowder arrives in a glass jar with housemade oyster crackers and bacon. (☏312-929-3501; www.gtoyster.com; 531 N Wells St, River North; mains $17-30; ☉5-10pm Mon-Thu, to 11pm Fri, 10am-2:30pm & 5-11pm Sat, 10am-2:30pm & 5-10pm Sun; Ⓜ Red Line to Grand)

Giordano's   PIZZA $$

12 ⓧ MAP P58, D2

Giordano's makes 'stuffed' pizza, a bigger, doughier version of deep dish. It's awesome. If you want a slice of heaven, order the 'special,' a stuffed pie containing sausage, mushroom, green pepper and onions. Each pizza takes 45 minutes to bake, so don't arrive starving. (☏312-951-0747; www.giordanos.com; 730 N Rush St, River North; small pizzas from $18; ☉11am-11pm Sun-Thu, to midnight Fri & Sat; Ⓜ Red Line to Chicago)

Gino's East   PIZZA $$

13 ⓧ MAP P58, D2

In the great deep-dish pizza wars, Gino's is easily one of the top-five heavies. And it encourages customers to do something wacky: cover every available surface – walls, chairs, staircases – with graffiti. The classic cheese-and-sausage pie oozes countless pounds of gooey goodness over a crispy golden crust. Prepare to wait for the pleasure as reservations are not accepted. (☏312-266-3337; www.ginoseast.com; 162 E Superior St, Streeterville; small pizzas from $18; ☉11am-9pm Sun-Thu, to 10pm Fri & Sat; Ⓜ Red Line to Chicago)

Topolobampo/ Frontera Grill   MEXICAN $$$

You've seen chef-owner Rick Bayless on TV, stirring pepper sauces and other jump-off-the-tongue Mexican creations. His isn't your typical taco menu: Bayless uses seasonal ingredients for his wood-grilled meats, flavor-packed mole sauces, chili-thickened braises and signature margaritas. Though they share space, Topolobampo and Frontera Grill, next door to Xoco (see 8 ⓧ Map P58, B4), are two separate restaurants: Michelin-starred Topolo is sleeker and pricier, while Frontera is more informal and reasonably priced. (☏312-661-1434; www.rickbayless.com; 445 N Clark St, River North; Topolo set menus $95-140, Frontera mains $22-35; ☉11:30am-10pm Tue-Thu, to 11pm Fri, 10:30am-11pm Sat; Ⓜ Red Line to Grand)

Drinking

Clark Street Ale House

BAR

14 🚇 MAP P58, B2

Do as the retro sign advises and 'Stop & Drink.' Midwestern microbrews are the main draw. Work up a thirst on the free pretzels, order a three-beer sampler for $7 and cool off in the beer garden out back. In a neighborhood where many bars lean toward pretentious, this is a great unassuming spot with an old-school vibe. (📞312-642-9253; www.clarkstreetalehouse.com; 742 N Clark St, River North; ⏰4pm-4am Mon-Fri, from 11am Sat & Sun; 🛜; Ⓜ Red Line to Chicago)

Centennial Chicago

Hiding in plain sight, **Centennial Crafted Beer & Eatery** (Map p58, B2; 📞312-284-5353; www.centennialchicago.com; 733 N LaSalle Dr, Near North; ⏰4pm-midnight Mon-Wed, 11:30am-midnight Thu, to 2am Fri, 10:30am-3am Sat, 10:30am-midnight Sun; Ⓜ Brown, Purple Line to Chicago) is rarely mobbed, like many of its neighborhood competitors. Its 50 taps of carefully chosen craft beer and its cozy, candelabra-and-weathered-wood vibe are exactly what you want in a bar. Beer lovers will never want to leave.

Second Story

GAY

15 🚇 MAP P58, D4

Climb the stairs that lead above Sayat Nova Armenian restaurant, and voilà, you've arrived at a friendly gay dive bar that most people don't even know is there. The wood-paneled walls, rainbow flags, disco ball and cheap drinks lend it a scruffy charm. Cash only. (📞312-923-9536; 157 E Ohio St, 2nd fl, Streeterville; ⏰noon-2am; Ⓜ Red Line to Grand)

Bar Ramone

WINE BAR

16 🚇 MAP P58, B4

A hodgepodge of funky light fixtures dangles from the ceiling, and paintings hang on the exposed-brick walls so the room resembles a salon. Settle in to a romantic table and choose from more than 25 wines available by the glass, including Txakolina, the sparkler from Spain's Basque region. Bar Ramone is perfect for a date night or after-dinner nightcap. (📞312-985-6909; www.barramone.com; 441 N Clark St, River North; ⏰4-10pm Sun & Mon, to 11pm Tue-Thu, to midnight Fri & Sat; Ⓜ Red Line to Grand)

Entertainment

Blue Chicago

BLUES

17 ⭐ MAP P58, B4

Commanding local acts wither the mikes nightly at this mainstream blues club. It's a pretty

Public Enemy Number One: Al Capone

Al Capone came to Chicago from New York in 1919. Prohibition fueled the success of the Chicago mob, which made fortunes dealing in illegal beer, gin and other intoxicants. Capone quickly moved up the ranks and was the city's mob boss from 1924 to 1931, until federal agent Eliot Ness – part of the 'The Untouchables' squad, whose members were supposedly impervious to bribes – brought him down on tax evasion charges.

Infamous Capone sites to see include the following:

Green Mill (p103) The speakeasy in the basement was a Capone favorite.

Holy Name Cathedral (Map p58, C2; ☎ 312-787-8040; www.holyname cathedral.org; 735 N State St, River North; Ⓜ Red Line to Chicago) Capone ordered a couple of hits that took place near the church.

Mt Carmel Cemetery Capone is buried in this cemetery in suburban Hillside, west of Chicago. His simple gravestone reads, 'Alphonse Capone, 1899–1947, My Jesus Mercy.'

St Valentine's Day Massacre Site (Map p87, E3; 2122 N Clark St, Lincoln Park; ☒ 22) Capone's thugs killed seven members of Bugs Moran's gang here. It's now a parking lot.

spartan setup, with a small, narrow room that gets packed. Arrive early to get a seat. While the crowd and River North environs are touristy, the bands are the real deal. (☎ 312-661-0100; www. bluechicago.com; 536 N Clark St, River North; tickets $10-12; ⊗ 8pm-1:30am Sun-Fri, to 2:30am Sat; Ⓜ Red Line to Grand)

Shopping

Garrett Popcorn
FOOD

18 🔒 MAP P58, D3

Patient crowds form long lines outside this popular popcorn store on the Magnificent Mile. Granted, the caramel popcorn is heavenly and the cheese popcorn decadent, but is it worth waiting in the cold, whipping snow for a chance to buy some? Actually, it is. Try the sumptuous Garrett Mix, which combines the two favourite flavors in one delicious and unforgettable treat. The entrance is situated on Ontario St. (www.gar rettpopcorn.com; 625 N Michigan Ave, Streeterville; ⊗ 10am-8pm Mon-Thu, to 9pm Fri & Sat, to 7pm Sun; Ⓜ Red Line to Grand)

Explore ✪
Gold Coast

The Gold Coast has been home to the wealthiest Chicagoans for well over a century. Bejeweled women glide through stylish boutiques as the occasional Tesla or Rolls-Royce wheels along the leafy streets. The 360° Chicago observatory and Museum of Contemporary Art are the top sights. At night, Rush St entertains with swanky steakhouses and piano lounges.

The Short List

○ *Signature Lounge (p69)* Soaring high in this 96th-floor lounge for tall drinks and sparkling views.

○ *Museum of Contemporary Art (p70)* Perusing the avant-garde artwork by day and an experimental theater performance at night.

○ *Astor Street (p79)* Ogling the genteel mansions where Chicago's rich and powerful have lived since the 1880s.

○ *International Museum of Surgical Science (p77)* Examining the eerie surgical instruments and fascinating exhibits at this esoteric museum.

Getting There & Around

Ⓜ Red Line to Clark/Division for the neighborhood's northern areas; Red Line to Chicago for the southern parts.

🚌 Number 151 runs along Michigan Ave, handy for further-flung sights.

🚗 Resident-only streets stymie street parking. Try LaSalle St, much of which is unmetered.

Neighborhood Map on p74

Gold Coast beaches TUPUNGATO/GETTY IMAGES ©

Top Sight 📷
360° Chicago

Located atop the city's fourth-tallest skyscraper, 875 N Michigan Ave, 360° Chicago is a dandy place to get high in Chicago. In many ways the view here surpasses the one at Willis Tower, as the building is closer to the lake and provides unfettered panoramic vistas. If that's not enough, the observatory offers a couple of thrill features as well.

◉ MAP P74, D7

📞 888-875-8439

www.360chicago.com

875 N Michigan Ave, 94th fl

adult/child $22/15

🕐 9am-11pm, last tickets 10:30pm

Ⓜ Red Line to Chicago

Observatory Lowdown

The 94th-floor observatory offers informative displays that tell you the names of the surrounding buildings. It has the **Skywalk**, a sort of screened-in porch that lets you feel the wind and hear the city sounds. The biggest draw is **Tilt** (pictured), a set of floor-to-ceiling windows that you stand in as they move and tip out over the ground; it costs $7.20 extra and is actually less spine-tingling than it sounds. The observatory is probably your best bet if you have kids or if you're a newbie and want to beef up your Chicago knowledge, but there are other options.

Architecture

The John Hancock Center, as the building was then known, was completed in 1969. Fazlur Khan and Bruce Graham were the chief architects, and they designed the structure to sway as much as 5in to 8in in Chicago's windy conditions. They went on to build the Willis Tower four years later.

Observatory Alternatives

Not interested in frivolities? Head straight for the building's 96th-floor **Signature Lounge** (www.signatureroom.com; ⏱11am-12:30am Sun-Thu, to 1:30am Fri & Sat), where the view is free if you buy a drink ($10 to $18). That's right, here you'll get a glass of wine and a comfy seat while staring out at almost identical views from a few floors higher than the observatory. The elevators for the lounge (and its companion restaurant on the 95th floor) are separate from those for the observatory. Look for signs that say 'Signature 95th/96th' one floor up from the observatory entrance.

★ Top Tips

◦ Go at night, when the views are particularly awesome. On Wednesday and Saturday evenings in summer there's the bonus of seeing Navy Pier's fireworks.

◦ Feel the speed as you ascend in the elevators. They're moving at 20mph.

◦ If you're short on time, this observatory is often less crowded than the one at Willis Tower.

✕ Take a Break

Join dapper residents from the neighboring high-rises for a Manhattan at the **Coq d'Or** (☏312-932-4623; 140 E Walton St; ⏱11am-1am Sun-Thu, to 2am Fri & Sat) lounge.

Hendrickx Belgian Bread Crafter (p78) hits the spot for waffles and other sweet treats.

Welcome to
the Commons

Top Sight 📷

Museum of Contemporary Art

In contrast to the classical collection of the Art Institute, the MCA exhibits contemporary, avant-garde works from the past century that often straddle the worlds of visual art and mixed media. Its modern photography collections are especially strong. With regularly changing displays, you're sure to see something unconventional, and maybe even controversial.

◎ MAP P74, E8

☏ 312-280-2660

www.mcachicago.org

220 E Chicago Ave

adult/child $15/free

🕙 10am-9pm Tue & Fri, to 5pm Wed, Thu, Sat & Sun

Ⓜ Red Line to Chicago

Exhibitions

The museum mounts themed exhibitions that typically focus on underappreciated or up-and-coming artists that curators are introducing to American audiences. For example, you might see the first US solo show of Brazilian documentary photographer Jonathas de Andrade, or 'multiphenate artist' Virgil Abloh's multimedia endeavors subverting high culture across the fields of fashion, architecture, graphic works and furniture design. Shows last three months or so before the galleries morph into something new.

Sculpture Garden & Front Plaza

The terraced sculpture garden at the back of the museum makes for a nifty browse. In summer (June through September) a jazz band plays amid the greenery every Tuesday at 5:30pm. Patrons bring blankets and sip drinks from the bar. The museum's front plaza also sees lots of action, especially on Tuesday mornings in June through October when a farmers market with veggies, cheeses and baked goods sets up from 7am to 2pm. Both events are big local to-dos.

Arty Theater

The Museum of Contemporary Art's theater regularly hosts dance, music and film events by contemporary A-listers. Much of it is pretty far out, eg an Inuit throat singer performing to a silent-film backdrop, a play about ventriloquists performed by a European puppet troupe, or nude male dancers leaping in a piece about how technology affects life. Bonus: a theater ticket stub provides free museum admission any time during the week after the show.

★ Top Tips

o Docents lead free, 45-minute tours through the galleries daily at 1pm, as well as weekends at 2pm. Meet at the 2nd-floor visitor service desk.

o Tuesdays are often crowded, as locals get free admission then.

o The museum shop wins big points for interesting books, unconventional gifts and jewelry and children's toys.

✕ Take a Break

Marisol, the MCA's stylish restaurant, serves locally sourced small plates, wines and aperitifs. It stays open beyond museum hours.

The city's most view-tastic bar is a few blocks away: the Signature Lounge (p69), found 96 floors up at 875 N Michigan Ave.

Walking Tour 🚶

Gold Coast Saunter

The name might clue you in: Chicago's wealthiest residents have called the Gold Coast home since the late 1800s. Bentleys sit parked outside elegant city mansions; fur-wearing women hobnob in stylish cafes. But hints of this posh neighborhood's quietly seamier side can also be found in between the wallet-busting boutiques and well-heeled restaurants.

Walk Facts

Start Newberry Library (M Red Line to Chicago)

End Lodge Tavern (M Red Line to Clark/Division)

Length 1.7 miles; two to three hours

❶ Newberry Library

Whether it's a map of Lewis and Clark's westward trek or a Shakespeare First Folio, the historic **Newberry Library** (p76) has it. Stop by for a free tour, check out the public galleries and browse the on-site bookstore, one of your best bets for Chicago-themed books.

❷ Washington Square

Across from Newberry Library is **Washington Square**, a park famed for its history of soapbox orators (often considered religious or political nuts, hence its nickname, 'Bughouse Square'). Local residents walk their dogs, workers eat lunch alfresco and crusty old-timers argue by the central fountain. It was added to the National Register of Historic Places in 1991.

❸ Oak Street

Moneyed locals stroll Oak Street to find a sleek Prada bag, a Harry Winston diamond or the perfect pair of Jimmy Choo pumps. (Everyone else comes to window-shop and sigh.) The designer boutiques line up in a pretty row between Michigan Ave and Rush St.

❹ 3 Arts Club Cafe

Pop into this sophisticated **cafe** (☎312-475-9116; www.3artscafe. com; 1300 N Dearborn St; ⏰10am-9pm Mon-Sat, 11am-7pm Sun; 🛜) for a light lunch, sitting on stylish couches in a sunny glass atrium replete with chandeliers, trees and a fountain. The original Three Arts Club, founded in 1912, was a home for women in the 'three arts' of music, painting and drama.

❺ Astor Street

Home to some of Chicago's richest denizens past and present, Astor Street was named for the USA's first multimillionaire, John Jacob Astor (he never lived there, but the area's builders thought his name added dazzle). Several turn-of-the-century mansions rise up between the 1300 and 1500 blocks.

❻ Original Playboy Mansion

This 1899 **mansion** (1340 N State Pkwy) was bought by Hugh Hefner at the start of the sexual revolution of the 1960s. It's all private condos now, so you can't go inside – but you can let your imagination run wild about the debauched carousing that once took place here in Hef's basement 'grotto' pool.

❼ Lodge Tavern

The woodsy **Lodge Tavern** (☎312-642-4406; www.lodgetavern.com; 21 W Division St; ⏰10am-4am Sun-Fri, to 5am Sat) has been catering to the Gold Coast's more downmarket crowd since 1957. Pick out an oldie on the Wurlitzer, grab a draft beer and share a free bowl of peanuts with the hard-drinking locals who hang out here until late.

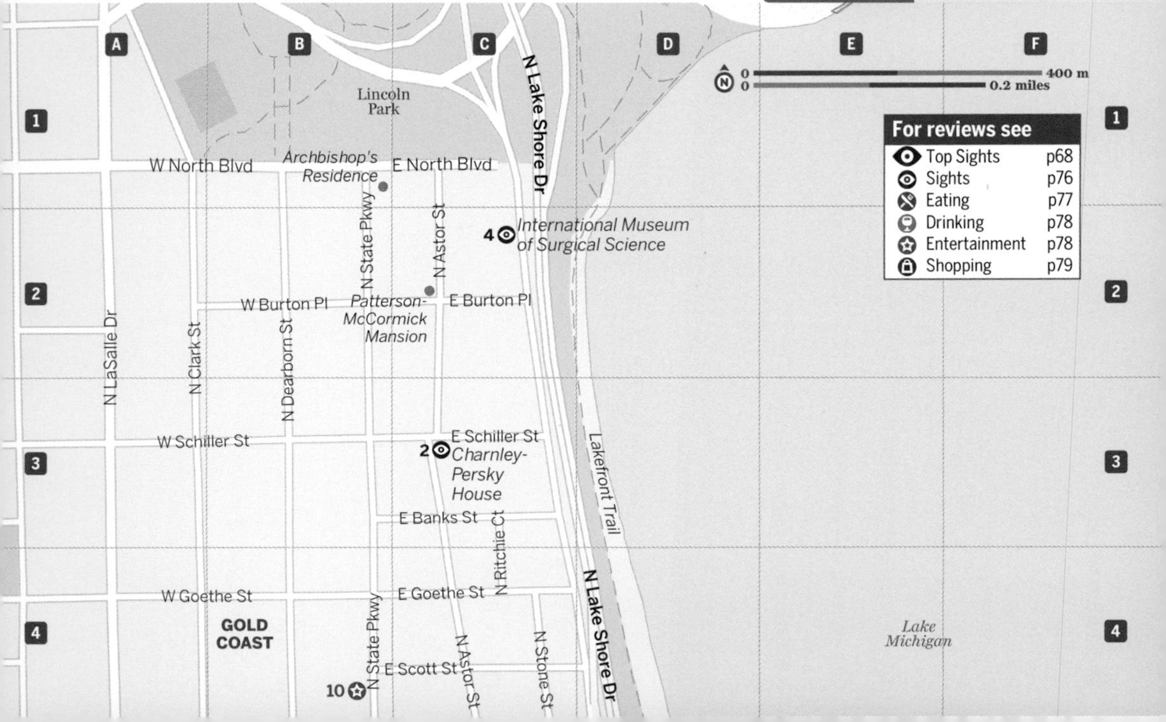

Gold Coast

For reviews see

◉ Top Sights p68
◉ Sights p76
✕ Eating p77
● Drinking p78
✪ Entertainment p78
🛍 Shopping p79

400 m
0.2 miles

Lake Michigan

Lakefront Trail

N Lake Shore Dr

N Lake Shore Dr

4 ◉ International Museum of Surgical Science

Lincoln Park

Archbishop's Residence

Patterson-McCormick Mansion

E North Blvd

W North Blvd

N Astor St

E Burton Pl

W Burton Pl

N State Pkwy

N Dearborn St

N Clark St

N LaSalle Dr

W Schiller St

W Goethe St

E Schiller St

2 ◉ Charnley-Persky House

E Banks St

N Ritchie Ct

E Goethe St

N Astor St

N Stone St

N State Pkwy

E Scott St

10 ✦

GOLD COAST

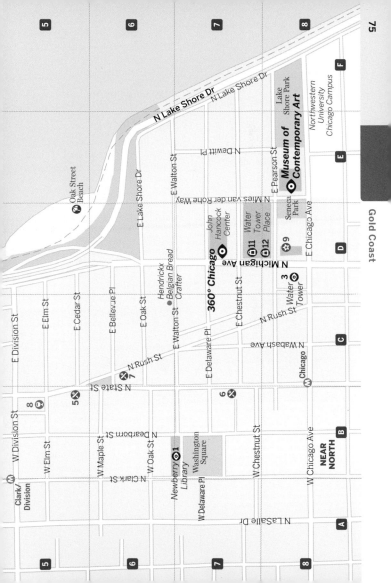

Gold Coast

Museum of Contemporary Art

Lake Shore Park

Northwestern University Chicago Campus

Oak Street Beach

N Lake Shore Dr

E Walton St

N Dewitt Pl

E Pearson St

Seneca Park

N Mies van der Rohe Way

John Hancock Center

Water Tower Place

E Chicago Ave

360° Chicago

Hendrickx Belgian Bread Crafter

N Michigan Ave

11

12

9

E Lake Shore Dr

E Walton St

E Oak St

E Bellevue Pl

E Cedar St

E Elm St

E Division St

E Delaware Pl

E Chestnut St

N Rush St

Water Tower

3

N Wabash Ave

Chicago

E Walton St

N State St

7

5

8

W Division St

W Elm St

Clark/ Division

N Dearborn St

W Maple St

W Oak St

Washington Square

Newberry Library

1

W Delaware Pl

N Clark St

N LaSalle Dr

6

W Chestnut St

W Chicago Ave

NEAR NORTH

Oak Street Beach

This **beach** (Map p74, D5; www.cpdbeaches.com; 1000 N Lake Shore Dr; ⏰6am-11pm; Ⓜ Red Line to Chicago) at the edge of downtown packs in bodies beautiful to play volleyball or sunbathe in the shadow of skyscrapers. Swimming is permitted in summer when lifeguards are on duty (11am to 7pm). You can rent umbrellas and lounge chairs. The island-themed, yellow-umbrella-dotted cafe provides drinks and DJs.

Sights

Newberry Library   LIBRARY

1 ◉ MAP P74, B7

The Newberry's public galleries are a treat for bibliophiles: those who swoon over original Thomas Paine pamphlets about the French Revolution, or get weak-kneed seeing Thomas Jefferson's copy of the *History of the Expedition under Captains Lewis and Clark* (with margin notes!). Intriguing exhibits rotate yellowed manuscripts and tattered 1st editions from the library's extensive collection. The on-site bookstore is tops for Chicago-themed titles. Free tours of the impressive building take place at 3pm Thursday and 10:30am Saturday. (☎312-943-9090; www.newberry.org; 60 W Walton St; admission free; ⏰galleries 8:15am-5pm Mon, Fri & Sat, to 7:30pm Tue-Thu; Ⓜ Red Line to Chicago)

Charnley-Persky House   ARCHITECTURE

2 ◉ MAP P74, C3

While he was still working for Louis Sullivan, Frank Lloyd Wright (who was 19 at the time) designed the 11-room Charnley-Persky House, which sparked a new era in architectural design. Why? Because it did away with Victorian gaudiness in favor of plain, abstract forms that went on to become the modern style. It was completed in 1892 and now houses the Society of Architectural Historians. (☎312-573-1365; www.charnleyhouse.org; 1365 N Astor St; tours Wed/Sat free/$10; ⏰noon Wed & Sat year-round, plus 10am Sat Apr-Oct; Ⓜ Red Line to Clark/Division)

Water Tower   LANDMARK

3 ◉ MAP P74, D8

This 154ft-tall turreted tower is a defining city icon: it was the sole downtown survivor of the 1871 Great Chicago Fire, thanks to its yellow limestone bricks, which withstood the flames. Today the tower houses the **City Gallery** (☎312-742-0808; admission free; ⏰10am-7pm Mon-Fri, to 5pm Sat & Sun), which is well worth a peek for its Chicago-themed works by local artists. (806 N Michigan Ave; Ⓜ Red Line to Chicago)

International Museum of Surgical Science

MUSEUM

4 MAP P74, C2

This small but fascinating museum, set inside a former residential mansion facing the lake, is dedicated to the world of surgery and medicine. Exhibits demonstrate the amazing strides made in medical science throughout history, on subjects as diverse as eyeglasses, wound healing, anesthesia and X-rays, as well as the history of nursing. Artifacts range from creaky old limb prosthetics and rather intimidating antique surgical instruments to an actual iron lung. (☎312-642-6502; www. imss.org; 1524 N Lake Shore Dr; adult/ child $17/9; ☉9:30am-5pm Mon-Fri, from 10am Sat & Sun; ☐151)

Eating

Velvet Taco

TACOS $

5 MAP P74, B5

An excellent late-night option for this area, Velvet Taco features hip new takes on the eminently adaptable taco: spicy chicken tikka; Nashville hot tofu with Napa slaw; shredded pork with avocado crema and grilled pineapple; Kobe bacon-burger with smoked cheddar; even shrimp and grits. Down a few accompanied by a margarita or a beer. (☎312-763-2654; www. velvettaco.com; 1110 N State St; tacos $3.50-7; ☉11am-midnight Mon, to 2am Tue & Wed, to 3am Thu, to 5am Fri, 10am-5am Sat, 10am-midnight Sun; ☑; ☐36, Ⓜ Red Line to Clark/ Division)

Oak Street Beach

Hendrickx Belgian Bread Crafter 🍴◎

Hiding in a nondescript apartment building, **Hendrickx Belgian Bread Crafter** (Map p74, C6; 📞 312-649-6717; www.hendrickxbakery.com; 100 E Walton St; mains $7-13; ⏱8am-7pm Tue-Sat, 9am-3pm Sun, 8am-3:30pm Mon; Ⓜ Red Line to Chicago) is a local secret. Push open the bright orange door and behold the waffles, brioche and croissants (in 12 flavors!), among other flaky, buttery, Belgian treats.

Pizano's   PIZZA $$

6 ❌ MAP P74, B7

Congenial Pizano's gets lost amid Chicago's pizza places, which is a shame since it's one of the best and has an illustrious pedigree (founded by Rudy Malnati Jr, whose dad created the deep-dish pizza, so the legend goes). The buttery crust impresses, even more so in its thin-crust incarnation. (Gluten-free crust is also available.) There's another Pizano's in the Loop (p50). (📞312-751-1766; www.pizanoschicago.com; 864 N State St; 10in pizzas from $16; ⏱11am-2am Sun-Fri, to 3am Sat; Ⓜ Red Line to Chicago)

Gibson's   STEAK $$$

7 ❌ MAP P74, C6

There's a scene every night at this local original. Politicians, movers, shakers and the shaken-down swirl the famed martinis and compete for prime table space in the buzzing dining room. The rich and beautiful mingle at the bar, often to live piano music. The steaks here are as good as they come, and ditto for the ginormous lobsters. (📞312-266-8999; www.gibsonssteakhouse.com; 1028 N Rush St; mains $24-63; ⏱11am-midnight; Ⓜ Red Line to Clark/Division)

Drinking

Sparrow   COCKTAIL BAR

8 🅿 MAP P74, B5

This refined lounge, inspired by hotel lobby bars of the 1930s and '40s, is a Gold Coast hidden gem. Tucked behind an unassuming storefront in an art deco apartment building, Sparrow emphasizes rum-focused cocktails, but there's also an extensive wine list and 10 rotating beers on tap. It's a great place to duck into after a nice dinner downtown. (📞312-725-0732; www.sparrowchicago.com; 12 W Elm St; ⏱4pm-2am Mon-Fri, to 3am Sat, to midnight Sun; Ⓜ Red Line to Clark/Division)

Entertainment

Lookingglass Theatre Company   THEATER

9 ⭐ MAP P74, D8

This well-regarded troupe works in a nifty theater hewn from the old **Water Works Pumping Station** building. The ensemble cast – which sometimes includes cofounder David Schwimmer of

TV's *Friends* – often uses physical stunts and acrobatics to enhance its dreamy, magical, literary productions. (📞312-337-0665; www.lookingglasstheatre.org; 821 N Michigan Ave; Ⓜ Red Line to Chicago)

Zebra Lounge   LIVE MUSIC

10 ⭐ MAP P74, B4

The piano in this tiny, dark and mirrored room – originally opened as a speakeasy during Prohibition – can get as scratchy as the voices of the crowd, which consists mainly of older folks who like to sing along. The ivory ticklers here are veterans who know their stuff. Live music starts at 9pm nightly. You'll find it in a residential building. (📞312-642-5140; www.thezebralounge.net; 1220 N State St; ⏰6pm-2am Mon-Fri, 7:30pm-3am Sat, 7:30pm-2am Sun; Ⓜ Red Line to Clark/Division)

Shopping

American Girl Place   TOYS

11 🔒 MAP P74, D7

This is not just a doll shop – it's an *experience*. Kids can create a completely customized doll that looks just like them, and even buy matching outfits. The cafe seats the dolls as part of the family during tea service. While there are American Girl stores in many cities, this flagship remains the largest and busiest. (📞877-247-5223; www.americangirl.com; 835 N Michigan Ave, Water Tower Place; ⏰10am-8pm Mon-Thu, to 9pm Fri, 9am-9pm Sat, 9am-6pm Sun; 👶; Ⓜ Red Line to Chicago)

Lego Store   TOYS

12 🔒 MAP P74, D8

After *ooohhing* and *aaahhing* at the cool models of rockets, castles and dinosaurs scattered throughout the store, kids can build their own designs at pint-sized tables equipped with bins of the signature little bricks. (📞312-202-0946; www.lego.com; 835 N Michigan Ave, 2nd fl, Water Tower Place; ⏰10am-9pm Mon-Sat, 11am-6pm Sun; 👶; Ⓜ Red Line to Chicago)

Astor Street   🔭

In the 1880s Chicago's rich and powerful families began moving to Astor St and trying to outdo each other with palatial homes. The mansions along the 1300 to 1500 blocks reflect the grandeur of that heady period. The **Patterson-McCormick Mansion** (Map p74, C2; 1500 N Astor St; 🚌151) is a neighborhood standout. New York architect Stanford White designed the 1893 neoclassical beauty, which is now divided into luxury condos. The 1885 **Archbishop's Residence** (Map p74, B1; 1555 N State Pkwy; 🚌72, 151) is another eye-popper, complete with 19 chimneys. The current archbishop does not live on-site, though the Catholic diocese still owns the building.

Explore
Lincoln Park & Old Town

Green space Lincoln Park is the city's premier playground, filled with lagoons, beaches and zoo animals. The same-name surrounding neighborhood adds top-notch restaurants, kicky shops and lively blues and rock clubs to the mix. To the south, stylish Old Town hangs on to its free-spirited, bohemian past with artsy bars and the improv-comedy bastion Second City.

The Short List

○ **Lincoln Park (p82)** *Meandering along the park's byways and hearing lions roar in the zoo, then discovering the calm of the hidden lily pool.*

○ **Second City (p92)** *Laughing, drinking and shouting out plot suggestions at this legendary comedy improv venue.*

○ **North Avenue Beach (p88)** *Enjoying fun in the sun with a jaunt on a kayak or stand-up paddleboard.*

○ **Steppenwolf Theatre (p92)** *Seeing a provocative play from the Pulitzer Prize–winning, star-filled ensemble.*

Getting There & Around

Ⓜ Brown, Purple, Red Line to Fullerton for Lincoln Park; Brown, Purple Line to Sedgwick for Old Town.

🚌 Number 151 along Michigan Ave.

🚗 Parking is difficult. In Old Town, try the pay garage at Piper's Alley, at North Ave and Wells St.

Neighborhood Map on p86

Top Sight 📷
Lincoln Park

Chicago's largest park (1200 acres) runs for 6 miles through the neighborhood that bears its name, from North Ave up to Diversey Pkwy (after which a sliver of it continues to the end of Lake Shore Dr). It's a favorite playground of locals, who flock here to stroll, picnic, sunbathe and play sports, as well as visit the eponymous zoo.

◎ MAP P86, G5

www.chicagoparkdistrict.com

🕑 6am-11pm

🚻

🚌 22, 151, 156

Zoo & Other Freebies

Opened in 1868, the free Lincoln Park Zoo (pictured; p88) has entertained generations of Chicagoans. Families swarm the grounds, which are smack in the park's midst. The Regenstein African exhibit lets you get close to pygmy hippos and dwarf crocodiles, while swingin' gorillas and chimps populate the Ape House and snow monkeys chill in the Macaque Forest. The leafy conservatory (p89) and hidden lily garden (p85) are also nearby – and free.

Lincoln & the Mausoleum

At the park's southern edge, sculptor Augustus Saint-Gaudens' **Standing Lincoln** (off W LaSalle Dr; 🚌22) shows the 16th US president deep in contemplation before giving a speech. Saint-Gaudens based the work on casts of Lincoln's face and hands made while Lincoln was alive. The statue stands behind the Chicago History Museum (p88).

Nearby, at the corner of LaSalle Dr and Clark St, take a gander at the **Couch Tomb** (off W LaSalle Dr; 🚌22). It's the sole remainder of the land's pre-1864 use as a municipal cemetery – which included burials of Confederate soldiers who died as prisoners of war at Camp Douglas, a Union stockade on the South Side of town. The city eventually relocated the bodies when Lincoln Park was created.

Beaches & Beyond

There's much more here beyond the zoo, gardens and monuments. Head north to find sailboat harbors, golf courses, bird sanctuaries and rowing clubs out gliding on the lagoons. Walk east from anywhere in the park and you'll come to the **Lakefront Trail**, which connects several beaches along the way.

★ Top Tips

• Markets and takeout joints pop up along Clark St and Diversey Pkwy, prime for picnic provisions.

• Convenient Divvy (p149) stations to hire a bike for a short ride are at the corner of Lake Shore Dr and North Blvd, at the Chicago History Museum and at the Theater on the Lake building (near the intersection of Lake Shore Dr and W Fullerton Pkwy).

• Visit the park on Wednesday or Saturday morning to browse the Green City Market (p93) bounty as a bonus.

✖ Take a Break

Sultan's Market (p91) offers heaping plates for a casual Middle Eastern meal.

The **J Parker** (📞312-254-4747; www.jparkerchicago. com; 1816 N Clark St, 13th fl; ⏰5pm-1am Mon-Thu, from 3pm Fri, from 11:30am Sat & Sun; 🚌22) provides a swanky break at its rooftop cocktail bar.

Walking Tour 🥾

Lincoln Park
for Families

Looking to entertain the little ones? A day in Lincoln Park will keep the whole family busy without breaking the bank. Generations of Chicagoans have been coming here to enjoy the greenery, the lakefront and the Lincoln Park Zoo, now one of the last free zoos in the country.

Walk Facts
Start Farm-in-the-Zoo (📱151, 156)

End Fullerton Beach (📱151, 156)

Length 2 miles; four to five hours

❶ Farm-in-the-Zoo

Start off at the big ol' barn at **Farm-in-the-Zoo** (www.lpzoo.org/exhibit/farm-zoo; 1911 North Stockton Dr; admission free; ⏱10am-5pm Mon-Fri, to 6:30pm Sat & Sun Jun-Aug, 10am-5pm Apr, May, Sep & Oct, 10am-4:30pm Nov-Mar), where kids can pet sheep, watch chicks hatch and learn how to milk a cow.

❷ Nature Boardwalk & Education Pavilion

Just north of there is the **Nature Boardwalk**, a half-mile path around the South Pond's wetlands ecosystem. Informational placards explain the marshy environment and the creatures that live there. The mod-looking arch you pass on the east side is the **Education Pavilion**. Local starchitect Jeanne Gang (of Aqua Tower fame) designed it; it's meant to resemble a turtle shell.

❸ RJ Grunts

All that walking will no doubt lead to rumbling bellies (and grumbling kiddos), so head out of the park and over to **RJ Grunts** (☎773-929-5363; www.rjgruntschicago.com; 2056 N Lincoln Park W; mains $11.50-22; ⏱11:30am-11pm Mon-Fri, from 10am Sat, 10am-9pm Sun; 👶) for lunch. The staff can store your stroller while you chow down on chocolate-peanut-butter-banana milkshakes and burgers. The menu, and the hubbub, are entirely kid-friendly.

❹ Lincoln Park Zoo

After lunch explore re-created geographical regions in the Regenstein African Journey and watch Ape House monkeys play at the two best exhibits at the **Lincoln Park Zoo** (p88).

❺ Alfred Caldwell Lily Pool

After strolling through the exhibits, continue north through the park and into the hidden oasis of the **Alfred Caldwell Lily Pool** (www.lincolnparkconservancy.org; 2391 N Stockton Dr; admission free; ⏱7:30am-dusk mid-Apr–mid-Nov), where you can sit and enjoy the serenity while your kids go on the lookout for turtles and dragonflies.

❻ Fullerton Beach

By now you've spent more than four hours in the park. If you have enough energy to continue, head east along Fullerton Pkwy to **Fullerton Beach**, where you can find a quiet patch of sand perfect for lazing in the sun and building castles. Plus, the curving headland offers one of the city's best skyline views – the ideal background for a keepsake family photo of your day.

A

B

Diversey

C

D

W Diversey Pkwy

W Diversey Pkwy

18 12

N Wayne Ave

N Lakewood Ave

N Magnolia Ave

N Lincoln Ave

N Sheffield Ave

N Halsted St

N Orchard St

N Clark St

10 19

W Wrightwood Ave

W Wrightwood Ave

Wrightwood

659

2

W Lill Ave

17

W Deming Pl

N Surrey Ct

N Racine Ave

N Seminary Ave

W Altgeld St

N Burling St

W Arlington Pl

W Montana St

Fullerton

W Fullerton Ave

LINCOLN PARK

N Janssen Ave

N Southport Ave

N Wayne Ave

N Lakewood Ave

N Racine Ave

N Clifton Ave

DePaul University

W Belden Ave

W Belden Ave

N Geneva Tce

9

W Webster Ave

N Magnolia Ave

N Seminary Ave

N Kenmore Ave

N Sheffield Ave

N Bissell St

N Fremont St

N Dayton St

N Halsted St

Oz Park

W Dickens Ave

W Armitage Ave

Armitage

W Cortland St

N Maud Ave

N Clybourn Ave

N Marcey St

N Kingsbury St

N Bissell St

W Wisconsin St

N Burling St

N Orchard St

N Howe St

N Larrabee St

W Willow St

N Elston Ave

North Branch Chicago River

W Willow St

N Dayton St

11

14

OLD TOWN

W North Ave

North/Clybourn

N Magnolia Ave

N Cherry Ave

N Kingsbury St

16

W Blackhawk St

N Halsted St

N Clybourn Ave

A

B

C

D

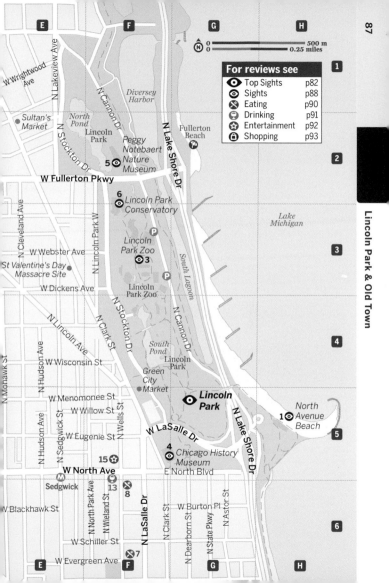

Lincoln Park & Old Town

E   F   G   H

N 0 ⟍‾‾‾‾‾‾‾‾‾‾⟍ 500 m
    0 ⟍‾‾‾‾‾‾‾‾‾‾⟍ 0.25 miles

1

For reviews see
◉ Top Sights   p82
◉ Sights   p88
✕ Eating   p90
◕ Drinking   p91
☆ Entertainment   p92
🔒 Shopping   p93

2

W Wrightwood Ave
N Lakeview Ave

Sultan's Market

N Lakeview Ave

N Cannon Dr

Diversey Harbor

Fullerton Beach

North Pond

Lincoln Park

Peggy Notebaert Nature Museum **5**◉

N Stockton Dr

W Fullerton Pkwy

6◉ Lincoln Park Conservatory

Lincoln Park Zoo

Lake Michigan

N Cleveland Ave

W Webster Ave

N Lincoln Park W

P

Lincoln Park Zoo ◉**3**

St Valentine's Day Massacre Site

W Dickens Ave

Lincoln Park Zoo

P

South Lagoon

N Cannon Dr

3

N Lincoln Ave

N Stockton Dr

W Wisconsin St

N Clark St

4

N Mohawk St

N Hudson Ave

South Pond

Lincoln Park

W Menomonee St

W Willow St

N Sedgwick St

N Wells St

Green City Market

Lincoln Park ◉

N Lake Shore Dr

W Eugenie St

N Hudson Ave

North Avenue Beach ◉**1**

5

W LaSalle Dr

15☆

W North Ave

Ⓜ Sedgwick

13◕

✕**8**

4◉ Chicago History Museum

E North Blvd

N LaSalle Dr

N Clark St

W Burton Pl

N Dearborn St

N State Pkwy

N Astor St

6

W Blackhawk St

N North Park Ave

N Wieland St

W Schiller St

W Evergreen Ave

✕**7**

E   F   G   H

Sights

North Avenue Beach · BEACH

1 ◉ MAP P86, H5

Chicago's most popular strand of sand gives off a bit of a Southern California vibe in summer. Buff teams spike volleyballs, kids build sandcastles and everyone jumps in for a swim when the weather heats up. Bands and DJs rock the steamboat-shaped beach house, which serves ice cream and margaritas in equal measure. Kayaks, Jet Skis, stand-up paddleboards, bicycles and lounge chairs are available to rent, and there are daily beach yoga classes. (www.cpdbeaches.com; 1600 N Lake Shore Dr, Lincoln Park; ⏱6am-11pm; 👫; 🚌151)

Wrightwood 659 · GALLERY

2 ◉ MAP P86, D2

Fans of modern architecture shouldn't miss Chicago's newest gallery, designed by Pritzker Prize–winner Tadao Ando. Walk past the facade of the former 1920s apartment building on a residential street and into a soaring four-story atrium of concrete and reclaimed brick; interior galleries on each floor are dedicated to rotating exhibits of architecture and 'socially engaged' art. (The inaugural exhibit covered previous works of Ando's and modern master Le Corbusier.) Reservations must be made online in advance; no walk-ins allowed. (☎773-437-6601; www.wrightwood659.org; 659 W Wrightwood Ave, Lincoln Park; $20; ⏱2-8:30pm Wed, from 10am Thu & Fri, 10am-5pm Sat; 🚌22)

Lincoln Park Zoo · ZOO

3 ◉ MAP P86, F3

The zoo has been around since 1868 and is a local freebie favorite, filled with lions, zebras, snow monkeys and other exotic creatures in the shadow of downtown. Check out the Regenstein African Journey, polar-bear-stocked Arctic Tundra and dragonfly-dappled Nature Boardwalk for the cream of the crop. The Gateway Pavilion (on Cannon Dr) is the main entrance; pick up a map and schedule of feedings and training sessions. (☎312-742-2000; www.lpzoo.org; 2200 N Cannon Dr, Lincoln Park; admission free; ⏱10am-5pm Mon-Fri, to 6:30pm Sat & Sun Jun-Aug, 10am-5pm Apr, May, Sep & Oct, 10am-4:30pm Nov-Mar; 👫; 🚌22, 151, 156)

Chicago History Museum · MUSEUM

4 ◉ MAP P86, F5

Curious about Chicago's storied past? Multimedia displays at this museum cover it all, from the Great Fire of 1871 to the 1968 Democratic Convention. President Lincoln's deathbed is here, as is the bell worn by Mrs O'Leary's cow. So is the chance to 'become' a Chicago hot dog covered in condiments (in the kids' area, but adults are welcome for the photo op). (📞312-642-4600; www.chicagohistory.org; 1601 N Clark St, Lincoln Park; adult/child $19/free; 🕑9:30am-4:30pm Mon & Wed-Sat, to 9pm Tue, noon-5pm Sun; ♿; 🚌22)

Peggy Notebaert Nature Museum   MUSEUM

5 ◎ MAP P86, F2

This hands-on museum has turtles and croaking frogs in its 1st-floor marsh, fluttering insects in its 2nd-floor butterfly haven and a bird boardwalk meandering through its rooftop garden. It's geared mostly to kids. Check the schedule for daily creature feedings. In winter the Green City Market (p93) sets up inside on Saturday morning. (📞773-755-5100; www.naturemuseum.org; 2430 N Cannon Dr; adult/child $9/6; 🕑9am-5pm Mon-Fri, from 10am Sat & Sun; ♿; 🚌76, 151)

Lincoln Park Conservatory   GARDENS

6 ◎ MAP P86, F2

Walking through the conservatory's 3 acres of desert palms, jungle ferns and tropical orchids is like taking a trip around the world in 30 minutes. Breathe in the Palm House, Fern Room, Orchid House and Show House, The glass-bedecked hothouse remains a sultry 75°F (24°C) escape even in winter. (📞312-742-7736; www.lincolnparkconservancy. org; 2391 N Stockton Dr, Lincoln Park; admission free; 🕑9am-5pm; 🚌151)

North Avenue Beach

Eating

Small Cheval
BURGERS **$**

7   MAP P86, F6

Upscale burger shack Small Cheval does one thing and does it well – it serves up delicious all-beef patties, with or without cheese, and a side of golden fries, accompanied by shakes, shots or beer (or if it's that kinda night, maybe all three). Enjoy your food on the picnic tables of the long front patio. There's another in Wicker Park (p110). (www.smallcheval.com; 1345 N Wells St, Old Town; burgers $9-10; 🕙11am-11pm Mon-Thu, to 1am Fri & Sat, to 10pm Sun; Ⓜ Red Line to Clark/Division)

La Fournette
BAKERY **$**

8   MAP P86, F6

The chef hails from France's Alsace region and he fills his narrow, rustic-wood bakery with bright-hued macarons (purple passionfruit, green pistachio, red raspberry-chocolate), cheese-infused breads, crust-crackling baguettes and buttery croissants. They all beg to be devoured on the spot with a cup of locally roasted Intelligentsia coffee. Staff make delicious soups, crepes, quiches and sandwiches with equal French love. (📞312-624-9430; www.lafournette.com; 1547 N Wells St, Old Town; baked goods $2-10; 🕙7am-6:30pm Mon-Sat, to 5:30pm Sun; Ⓜ Brown, Purple Line to Sedgwick)

Pequod's Pizza
PIZZA **$**

9   MAP P86, A3

Like the ship in *Moby Dick* from which this neighborhood restaurant takes its name, Pequod's pan-style (akin to deep-dish) pizza is a thing of legend – head and shoulders above chain competitors for its caramelized cheese, generous toppings and sweetly flavored sauce. Neon beer signs glow from the walls, and Blackhawks jerseys hang from the ceiling in the affably rugged interior. (📞773-327-1512; www.pequodspizza.com; 2207 N Clybourn Ave, Lincoln Park; small pizzas from $12; 🕙11am-2am Mon-Sat, to midnight Sun; 🚌9 to Webster)

Wieners Circle
AMERICAN **$**

10   MAP P86, D1

As famous for its unruly, foul-mouthed ambience as for its charred hot dogs and cheddar fries, the Wieners Circle is a

---

Sightseeing from the L

The L (short for 'elevated') train provides a great cheap sightseeing tour of the city. For the best views, hop on the Brown Line and ride into the Loop. Get on in Lincoln Park at either the Fullerton or Armitage stops, take a seat by the window and watch as the train clatters downtown, swinging past skyscrapers so close you can almost touch them.

normal hot-dog stand – with damn good food – daytimes and week-nights. The wild show comes week-end nights around 2am, when the nearby bars close and everyone starts yelling. The F-bombs fly and it can get raucous between staff and customers. (📞773-477-7444; 2622 N Clark St, Lincoln Park; hot dogs $3.50-5.50; 🕙11am-4am Sun-Thu, to 5am Fri & Sat; Ⓜ Brown, Purple Line to Diversey)

Alinea   GASTRONOMY $$$

11 🍴 MAP P86, D5

One of the world's best restau-rants, the triple-Michelin-starred Alinea purveys multiple courses of molecular gastronomy. Dishes may emanate from a centrifuge or be pressed into a capsule, à la duck served with a 'pillow of lavender air.' There are no reservations; instead Alinea sells tickets two to three months in advance via its website. Check Twitter (@Alinea) for last-minute seats. (📞312-867-0110; www.alinearestaurant.com; 1723 N Halsted St, Old Town; 10-/16-course menus from $205/290; 🕙5-10pm; Ⓜ Red Line to North/Clybourn)

Drinking

Delilah's   BAR

12 🍺 MAP P86, B1

A bartender rightfully referred to this hard-edged black sheep of the neighborhood as the 'pride of Lincoln Ave': a title earned for the heavy pours and the best whiskey selection in the city – over 860 dif-

Sultan's Market

Neighborhood folks dig into plates heaped with falafel sandwiches, creamy hum-mus, lamb shawarma, spinach pies and other quality Middle Eastern fare at family-run **Sultan's Market** (Map p86, E2; 📞872-253-1489; 2521 N Clark St, Lincoln Park; mains $4-10; 🕙10am-10pm Mon-Sat, to 9pm Sun; 🍴; Ⓜ Brown, Purple, Red Line to Fullerton). There's a large salad bar, too. The small, homey space doesn't have many tables, but Lincoln Park is nearby for picnicking.

ferent labels! The no-nonsense staff know their way around a beer list, too, tapping unusual domestic and international suds. Cheap Pabst longnecks are always available. (📞773-472-2771; www.delilahschicago.com; 2771 N Lincoln Ave, Lincoln Park; 🕙4pm-2am Sun-Fri, to 3am Sat; Ⓜ Brown Line to Diversey)

Old Town Ale House   BAR

13 🍺 MAP P86, F5

Located near the Second City (p92) comedy club and the scene of late-night musings since the 1960s, this unpretentious neighborhood fa-vorite lets you mingle with beautiful people and grizzled regulars, seated pint by pint under the paintings of nude politicians (just go with it). Classic jazz on the jukebox provides the soundtrack for the jovial goings-on. Cash only. (📞312-944-7020; www.theoldtownalehouse.com; 219 W North Ave, Old Town; 🕒3pm-4am Mon-Fri, noon-5am Sat, noon-4am Sun; Ⓜ️Brown, Purple Line to Sedgwick)

Entertainment

Steppenwolf Theatre   THEATER

14 ⭐ MAP P86, C5

Steppenwolf is Chicago's top stage for quality, provocative theater productions. The Hollywood-heavy ensemble includes Gary Sinise, John Malkovich, Martha Plimpton, Gary Cole, Joan Allen and Tracy Letts. A money-saving tip: the box office releases 20 tickets for $20 for each day's shows; they go on sale at 11am Tuesday to Saturday and at 1pm Sunday, and are avail-

able by phone. (📞312-335-1650; www.steppenwolf.org; 1650 N Halsted St, Lincoln Park; 🕒box office 11am-6:30pm Tue-Sat, from 1pm Sun; Ⓜ️Red Line to North/Clybourn)

Second City   COMEDY

15 ⭐ MAP P86, F5

Bill Murray, Stephen Colbert, Tina Fey and more honed their wit at this slick venue with nightly shows. The Mainstage and ETC stage host sketch revues (with an improv scene thrown in); they're similar in price and quality. If you turn up around 10pm Monday through Thursday (or 1am Saturday or 9pm Sunday) you can watch a free improv set. (📞312-337-3992; www.secondcity.com; 1616 N Wells St, Old Town; tickets $35-55; Ⓜ️Brown, Purple Line to Sedgwick)

Steppenwolf Theatre

iO Theater
COMEDY

16 ⭐ MAP P86, C6

One of Chicago's top-tier (and original) improv houses, iO is a bit edgier (and cheaper) than its competition, with four stages hosting bawdy shows of regular and musical improv nightly. Two bars and a beer garden add to the fun. The Improvised Shakespeare Company is awesome; catch them if you can. (📞312-929-2401; www.ioimprov.com; 1501 N Kingsbury St, Lincoln Park; tickets $5-16; Ⓜ Red Line to North/Clybourn)

BLUES
BLUES

17 ⭐ MAP P86, D2

Long, narrow and high volume, this veteran blues club draws a slightly older crowd that soaks up every crackling, electrified moment. As one local musician put it, 'The audience here comes out to *understand* the blues.' Big local names grace the small stage. (📞773-528-1012; www.chicagobluesbar.com; 2519 N Halsted St, Lincoln Park; cover charge $5-10; 🕐8pm-2am Wed-Sun; Ⓜ Brown, Purple, Red Line to Fullerton)

Shopping

Rotofugi
TOYS

18 🔒 MAP P86, B1

Rotofugi has an unusual niche: urban designer toys. The spacey, roboty, odd vinyl and plush items will certainly distinguish you from the other kids on the block. It's also a gallery showcasing artists in the fields of modern pop and illustration art. You can usually find locally

Green City Market

Stands of purple cabbages, red radishes, green asparagus and other bright-hued produce sprawl through Lincoln Park at Chicago's biggest **farmers market** (Map p86, F5; 📞773-880-1266; www.greencitymarket.org; 1790 N Clark St, Lincoln Park; 🕐7am-1pm Wed & Sat May-Oct; 🚌22). Follow your nose to the demonstration tent, where local cooks such as *Top Chef* winner Stephanie Izard prepare dishes using market ingredients.

designed Shawnimals here – cute critters from the mind of Chicago artist Shawn Smith. (📞773-868-3308; www.rotofugi.com; 2780 N Lincoln Ave, Lincoln Park; 🕐11am-7pm Mon-Fri, 10am-6pm Sat & Sun; Ⓜ Brown, Purple Line to Diversey)

Dave's Records
MUSIC

19 🔒 MAP P86, D1

Rolling Stone magazine picked Dave's as one of the nation's best record stores. It has an 'all vinyl, all the time' mantra, meaning crate diggers will be in their element flipping through the stacks of rock, jazz, blues, folk and house. Dave himself usually mans the counter, where you'll find a slew of 25¢ cheapie records for sale. (📞773-929-6325; www.davesrecordschicago.com; 2604 N Clark St; 🕐11am-8pm Mon-Sat, noon-7pm Sun; Ⓜ Brown, Purple Line to Diversey)

Explore ◈
Lake View & Wrigleyville

Good-time neighborhood Lake View is known for its nonstop lineup of bars, theaters, rock halls and global eateries. Wrigleyville is the pocket that surrounds star attraction Wrigley Field, where new cocktail bars, fancy doughnut shops and trendy eateries have joined the game. The rainbow banners of Boystown flutter next door, home to gay bars and dance clubs.

The Short List

∘ ***Wrigley Field (p96)*** *Spending an afternoon in the bleachers, hot dog and beer in hand, hoping for a win at the ivy-clad home of the Cubs.*

∘ ***Metro (p101)*** *Hearing a soon-to-be-famous band at Chicago's premier loud-rock venue, a tastemaker for more than three decades.*

∘ ***Boystown (p99)*** *Joining the thumping nightlife amid the rainbow flags in the city's main gay neighborhood.*

∘ ***Global eats (p99)*** *Chowing on Korean fried chicken, Filipino cakes, Thai noodles and more in the array of reasonably priced international restaurants, such as Gundis Kurdish Kitchen.*

Getting There & Around

Ⓜ Red Line to Addison for Wrigleyville and around; Red, Brown, Purple Line to Belmont for much of Boystown.

🚃 Number 77 plies Belmont Ave.

🚗 Parking is a nightmare, especially in Wrigleyville, where side streets are resident-only. Take the train!

Neighborhood Map on p98

Chicago Cubs pitcher, Yu Darvish, at Wrigley Field (p96)

Top Sight 📷
Wrigley Field

Built in 1914, Wrigley Field – aka the Friendly Confines – is the second-oldest baseball park in the major leagues. It's filled with legendary traditions and curses, including a team that didn't win a championship for 108 years. But a World Series victory coupled with heaps of new family-friendly and foodie hot spots around the stadium have given it new life.

◎ MAP P98, B3

📞 800-843-2827

www.cubs.com

1060 W Addison St, Wrigleyville

Ⓜ Red Line to Addison

Environs

The ballpark provides an old-school slice of Americana, with a hand-turned scoreboard, ivy-covered outfield walls and an iconic neon sign over the front entrance. The field is uniquely situated smack in the middle of a neighborhood, surrounded on all sides by houses, bars and restaurants. The grassy plaza just north of the main entrance – aka **Gallagher Way** (www.gallagherway.com; 3637 N Clark St, Wrigleyville) – has tables, chairs, a coffee shop and a huge video screen.

The Curse & Its Reverse

It started with Billy Sianis, owner of the Billy Goat Tavern. In 1945, the Cubs were in the World Series against the Detroit Tigers. When Sianis tried to enter Wrigley Field with his pet goat to see the game, ballpark staff refused, saying the goat stank. Sianis threw up his arms and called down a mighty hex, saying that the Cubs would never win another World Series. Years rolled by, and they didn't. Then in 2016 it happened: the Cubs won the Series in a wild, come-from-behind set of games. The curse was exorcised. At the victory parade a few days later, an estimated five million fans partied with the team.

Local Traditions

When the middle of the seventh inning arrives, it's time for the seventh-inning stretch. You then stand up for the group sing-along of 'Take Me Out to the Ballgame,' often led by a guest celebrity along the lines of Mr T, Ozzy Osbourne or the local weather reporter. Here's another tradition: if you catch a home run slugged by the competition, you're honor-bound to throw it back onto the field.

★ Top Tips

o Buy tickets at the Cubs' website or Wrigley box office. Online ticket broker StubHub (www.stubhub.com) is also reliable.

o The Upper Reserved Infield seats are usually pretty cheap. They're high up, but have decent views.

o Ninety-minute stadium tours ($25) are available most days April through September. Try going on a non-game day, as you'll see more.

✕ Take a Break

It's a pre-game ritual to beer up at **Murphy's Bleachers** (📞773-281-5356; www.murphysbleachers.com; 3655 N Sheffield Ave, Wrigleyville; ⏰11am-2am), only steps away from the ballpark.

For a taste of the new Wrigley scene, order a rare whiskey at Mordecai (p100) and angle for a seat on the terrace.

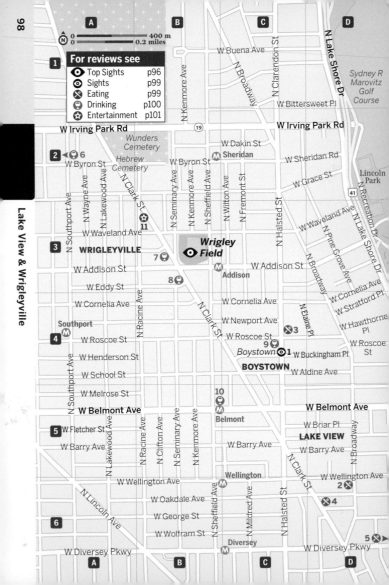

For reviews see

◉	Top Sights	p96
◉	Sights	p99
✖	Eating	p99
🍷	Drinking	p100
✪	Entertainment	p101

0 — 400 m
0 — 0.2 miles

W Buena Ave
W Bittersweet Pl
Sydney R Marovitz Golf Course

W Irving Park Rd
W Irving Park Rd

Wunders Cemetery
Hebrew Cemetery

W Dakin St
Sheridan
W Sheridan Rd
Lincoln Park

W Byron St
W Byron St
W Grace St

W Waveland Ave

WRIGLEYVILLE
W Waveland Ave

Wrigley Field

W Addison St
Addison
W Addison St

W Eddy St

W Cornelia Ave
W Cornelia Ave
W Cornelia Ave
W Stratford Pl

Southport
W Roscoe St
W Newport Ave
W Hawthorne Pl

W Henderson St
W Roscoe St
W Roscoe St

W School St
Boystown ◉1
W Buckingham Pl

BOYSTOWN
W Aldine Ave

W Melrose St

W Belmont Ave
W Belmont Ave
Belmont
W Briar Pl

LAKE VIEW

W Fletcher St
W Barry Ave
W Barry Ave

W Barry Ave
W Barry Ave

Wellington
W Wellington Ave

W Wellington Ave
W Oakdale Ave

W George St

W Wolfram St

Diversey
W Diversey Pkwy
W Diversey Pkwy

Sights

Boystown
AREA

1 MAP P98, C4

What the Castro is to San Francisco, Boystown is to the Windy City. The mecca of queer Chicago (especially for men), the streets of Boystown are full of rainbow flags and packed with bars, shops and restaurants catering to residents of the gay neighborhood. (btwn Halsted St & Broadway, Belmont Ave & Addison St, Boystown; M Red Line to Addison)

Eating

Crisp
KOREAN $

2 MAP P98, D6

Music blasts from the stereo while delicious Korean fusions arrive from the kitchen at this cheerful little spot. The 'Bad Boy Buddha' bowl, a variation on *bibimbap* (mixed vegetables with rice), is one of the best healthy lunches in town. Crisp's fried chicken (especially the 'Seoul Sassy' with its savory soy-ginger sauce) also wows the casual crowd. (773-697-7610; www.crisponline.com; 2940 N Broadway, Lake View; mains $8-14; 11:30am-9pm; M Brown, Purple Line to Wellington)

Chicago Diner
VEGETARIAN $

3 MAP P98, C4

It's the gold standard for Chicago vegetarians and a longtime favorite, as the 'meat-free since '83' tagline indicates. Top marks go to the mushroom lentil loaf (a truffle-sauced take on meatloaf), Radical Reuben (using corned beef seitan) and milkshakes (made with vegan ice cream and soy milk). Bright-red tables, hard-back booths and counter stools provide a vintage diner ambience. (773-935-6696; www.veggiediner.com; 3411 N Halsted St, Boystown; 11am-10pm Mon-Thu, to 11pm Fri, 10am-11pm Sat, 10am-10pm Sun; ; M Red Line to Addison)

Gundis Kurdish Kitchen
KURDISH $$

4 MAP P98, D6

The owners, who hail from southern Turkey, prepare meals from their Kurdish homeland. Dishes include *sac tawa,* a traditional stir-fry of meat, peppers and tomatoes on a sizzling plate, and *tirsik,* a stew of eggplant, carrots and other veggies in a spicy sauce. Sunshine streams into the airy, exposed-brick room by day, while pendant lights create a romantic vibe at night. (773-904-8120; www.thegundis.com; 2909 N Clark St, Lake View; mains $17-26; 9am-9pm Mon, Wed & Thu, to 10pm Fri & Sat, to 8pm Sun; M Brown, Purple Line to Wellington)

mfk
SPANISH $$

5 MAP P98, D6

In mfk's teeny space it feels like you're having a romantic meal at the seaside in Spain. Dig into crunchy prawn heads, garlicky octopus and veal meatballs amid the whitewashed walls and decorative

Game Day Crowds

If there's a Cubs game at Wrigley Field, plan on around 30,000 extra people joining you for a visit to the neighborhood. The trains and buses will be stuffed to capacity, traffic will be snarled, and bars and restaurants will be packed to the rafters. Visit on a non-game day for a bit more elbow room.

tiles. Sunny cocktails and a wine list dominated by whites and rosés add to the goodness. The restaurant is named after food writer MFK Fisher, a foodie well before her time. (☏773-857-2540; www.mfkrestaurant.com; 432 W Diversey Pkwy, Lake View; small plates $10-20; ⏰5-10pm Tue, noon-10pm Wed, Thu & Sun, noon-midnight Fri & Sat; 🚌22)

Drinking

Ten Cat Tavern   PUB

6 🚇 MAP P98, A2

Pool is serious business on the two vintage tables that the pub refelts regularly with Belgian material. The ever-changing, eye-catching art comes courtesy of neighborhood artists and the furniture is a garage saler's dream. Regulars (most in their 30s) down leisurely drinks at the bar or, in warm weather, in the beer garden. The back room has a toasty fireplace. (☏773-935-5377; 3931 N Ashland Ave, Lake View; ⏰3pm-2am; 🚇Brown Line to Irving Park)

Mordecai   COCKTAIL BAR

7 🚇 MAP P98, B3

Early-20th-century Cubs baseball great Mordecai Brown lends his name to this stylish bar at Hotel Zachary. With a serious cocktail menu spotlighting vintage whiskeys, it's a far cry from Wrigleyville's standard sticky-floored boozers. Snacks like beer-battered cheese curds dusted with bonito and *togarashi* spice play wonderfully with high and low cuisine. Opens three hours prior to Cubs home games. (☏773-269-5410; www.mordecai chicago.com; 3632 N Clark St, Wrigleyville; ⏰5-11pm Sun-Thu, to midnight Fri & Sat; 🚇Red Line to Addison)

Smart Bar   CLUB

Smart Bar is a long-standing, unpretentious favorite for dancing, located in the basement of the Metro (see 11 ⭐ Map p98, B3) rock club. The DJs are often more renowned than you'd expect the intimate space to accommodate. House and techno dominate the turntables. (☏773-549-4140; www.smartbarchicago.com; 3730 N Clark St, Wrigleyville; tickets $5-15; ⏰10pm-4am Thu, Fri & Sun, to 5am Sat; 🚇Red Line to Addison)

Sluggers   SPORTS BAR

8 🚇 MAP P98, B3

Practice your home-run swing at Sluggers, a cheesy but popular bar and grill across from Wrigley Field. Sidestep the schnockered Cubs fans and giant-screen TVs and head to the 2nd floor, where there are four batting cages. Ten pitches cost $2. (☏773-472-9696; www.sluggersbar.com; 3540 N Clark St, Wrigleyville; ⏱11am-2am Sun-Fri, to 3am Sat; Ⓜ Red Line to Addison)

Roscoe's Tavern
GAY

9 Ⓣ MAP P98, C4

Roscoe's has been bringing in the Boystown crowd for more than three decades. Different parts of the venue have different vibes: a casual bar in front, a dance club in back and a sun-splashed patio outdoors. Drag-race viewing parties, karaoke and dueling piano events are sprinkled throughout the week. (☏773-281-3355; www.roscoes.com; 3356 N Halsted St, Boystown; ⏱5pm-2am Mon-Thu, noon-2am Fri & Sun, noon-3am Sat; Ⓜ Red, Brown, Purple Line to Belmont)

Berlin
CLUB

10 Ⓣ MAP P98, B5

Looking for a packed, sweaty dance floor that's loads of fun? Berlin caters to a mostly gay crowd midweek, though partiers of all stripes jam the place on weekends. Monitors flicker through the latest video dispatches from cult pop and electronic acts, while DJs take the dance floor on trancey detours. There's a $10 cover charge on Friday and Saturday. (☏773-348-4975; www.berlinchicago.com; 954 W Belmont Ave, Lake View; ⏱10pm-2am Mon, to 4am Tue-Thu & Sun, 8pm-4am Fri, 8pm-5am Sat; Ⓜ Red, Brown, Purple Line to Belmont)

Entertainment

Metro
LIVE MUSIC

11 ⭐ MAP P98, B3

For more than three decades, the Metro has been synonymous with loud rock. Sonic Youth and the Ramones in the '80s. Nirvana and Jane's Addiction in the '90s. White Stripes and the Killers in the new millennium. Each night prepare to hear noise by three or four bands who may well be teetering on the verge of stardom. The venue remains a draw for the biggest acts, while maintaining an intimate atmosphere. (☏773-549-4140; www.metrochicago.com; 3730 N Clark St, Wrigleyville; ⏱box office noon-6pm Mon, to 8pm Tue-Sat; Ⓜ Red Line to Addison)

Fitz and the Tantrums at the Metro

Worth a Trip

Strolling Andersonville & Uptown

The formerly Swedish enclave of Andersonville is a vibrant neighborhood where long-standing businesses mix with new foodie restaurants, antique shops and gay bars. Adjacent Uptown is a whole different scene, with historic jazz houses such as the Green Mill and the popular restaurants of 'Little Saigon.' Both areas are prime for strolling, window-shopping, eating and drinking.

Getting There

Ⓜ Red Line to Berwyn. (Other Red Line stops in the area include Argyle and Lawrence.)

🚌 Number 22 up Clark St.

❶ Big Jones

The 'Southern heirloom cooking' at airy **Big Jones** (📞773-275-5725; www.bigjoneschicago.com; 5347 N Clark St, Andersonville; mains $14-29; ⏰11am-9pm Mon-Thu, to 10pm Fri, 9am-10pm Sat, 9am-9pm Sun) offers popular draws likes crawfish étouffée and shrimp and grits. Locals flock here on weekend mornings for an indulgent brunch.

❷ Lost Larson

Design-forward bakery **Lost Larson** (📞773-944-0587; www.lostlarson.com; 5318 N Clark St, Andersonville; baked goods $4.50-7; ⏰7am-7pm Wed-Sun) harks back to Andersonville's immigrant past with Scandinavian pastries like cardamom buns and lingonberry-almond cake. The chocolate croissant alone is worth the trip.

❸ Andersonville Galleria

Several dozen kiosks of locally made art, crafts and food spread over three floors at the **Andersonville Galleria** (📞773-878-8570; www.andersonvillegalleria.com; 5247 N Clark St, Andersonville; ⏰11am-7pm Mon-Sat, to 6pm Sun). Support local artisans while finding that perfect gift.

❹ Woolly Mammoth

Satisfy your morbid leanings at **Woolly Mammoth Antiques & Oddities** (📞773-989-3294; www.woollymammothchicago.com; 1513 W Foster Ave, Uptown; ⏰noon-7pm Wed-Sun, from 1pm Mon, from 3pm Tue), stuffed with all manner of the macabre: creepy doll heads, taxidermied animals and more.

❺ Hot 'G' Dog

Hot 'G' Dog (📞773-209-3360; www.hotgdog.com; 5009 N Clark St, Uptown; hot dogs $3-5, specialty sausages $7.50-9; ⏰10:30am-8pm Mon-Sat, to 4pm Sun; 🖍) is the place to sample, say, a chicken-apple-cranberry hot dog with whiskey cheese and pecans. Feeling a bit less gourmet? Go for a good ol' Chicago-style dog.

❻ Nha Hang Vietnam

Humble **Nha Hang Vietnam** (📞773-878-8895; 1032 W Argyle St, Uptown; mains $8-14; ⏰8:30am-10pm Mon & Wed-Sat, to 9pm Sun) dazzles with delicious, authentically made dishes. Try the steaming-hot pho or the clay-pot catfish.

❼ Big Chicks

Iconic **Big Chicks** (📞773-728-5511; www.bigchicks.com; 5024 N Sheridan Rd, Uptown; ⏰4pm-2am Mon-Fri, from 8:30am Sat, from 10am Sun; 📶) is a mainstay of the Chicago queer community, though it's open to all. Stop by for DJs, dancing and a welcoming vibe.

❽ Green Mill

The timeless **Green Mill** (📞773-878-5552; www.greenmilljazz.com; 4802 N Broadway, Uptown; ⏰noon-4am Mon-Fri, to 5am Sat, 11am-4am Sun) earned its notoriety as Al Capone's favorite speakeasy. Sit in one of the curved leather booths and enjoy nightly jazz performances.

Explore ⊕

Wicker Park, Bucktown & Ukrainian Village

Hipster record stores, vintage shops and cocktail lounges have shot up around these three West Town neighborhoods, though old-school dive bars linger on side streets. Wicker Park is the more commercial heart; Bucktown is a bit posher and Ukrainian Village a bit shabbier. The restaurant and rock-club scene around here is unparalleled in the city.

The Short List

o *Milwaukee Ave (p113)* Trawling for treasures in the vintage shops between Damen and Ashland Aves, such as Una Mae's.

o *Hideout (p111)* Snapping your fingers to a poetry slam or singing along with a Meatloaf tribute band in one of Chicago's coolest venues.

o *606 (p108)* Strolling on high through the neighborhood past hip restaurants and locals' backyards via this elevated trail.

o *Quimby's (p112)* Perusing the zines and getting the lowdown on the city's underground culture.

Getting There & Around

Ⓜ Blue Line to Damen or Division for Bucktown and Wicker Park; to Chicago for Ukrainian Village.

🚌 Lines number 50, 66, 70 72, and 73 service the area.

🚗 On-street parking is at a premium in Wicker Park and Bucktown.

Neighborhood Map on p106

Wicker Park RICHARD WEBER/ALAMY STOCK PHOTO ©

Wicker Park, Bucktown & Ukrainian Village

For reviews see

⊙ Sights	p108
✕ Eating	p108
◑ Drinking	p111
🎭 Entertainment	p111
🛍 Shopping	p112

0.5 miles

1 km

BUCKTOWN

WICKER PARK

Sights

Intuit: The Center for Intuitive & Outsider Art   GALLERY

1 ◉ MAP P106, F7

Behold this small museum's collection of naive and outsider art from Chicago artists, including rotating mixed-media exhibits and watercolors by famed local Henry Darger. In a back room the museum has re-created Darger's awesomely cluttered studio apartment, complete with balls of twine, teetering stacks of old magazines, an ancient typewriter and a Victrola phonograph. The gift shop carries groovy jewelry (such as pencil-eraser necklaces), bags and wallets made from recycled material, and art books. (📞312-243-9088; www.art.org; 756 N Milwaukee Ave, River West; $5; ⊙11am-6pm Tue,

---

The 606 Trail

Like NYC's High Line, Chicago's **606** (Map p106, B3; www.the606.org; Wicker Park/Bucktown; ⊙6am-11pm; Ⓜ Blue Line to Damen) is a similar urban-cool elevated path along an old train track. Bike or stroll past factories, smokestacks, clattering L trains and locals' backyard affairs for 2.7 miles between Wicker Park and Logan Square. The trail parallels Bloomingdale Ave, with access points every quarter mile.

Wed, Fri & Sat, to 7pm Thu, noon-5pm Sun; Ⓜ Blue Line to Chicago)

Document Gallery   GALLERY

2 ◉ MAP P106, C7

Document organizes exhibitions of contemporary photography, film and media-based works by emerging national and international artists. It shares its large space with three other galleries – Western Exhibitions, P•L•HK and Volume Gallery – and its stretch of Chicago Ave holds quite a few more art showrooms to boot. Stroll from 1400 to 2300 W Chicago Ave for further gallery explorations. (📞262-719-3500; www.documentspace.com; 1709 W Chicago Ave, West Town; ⊙11am-6pm Tue-Sat; 🚌66, Ⓜ Blue Line to Chicago)

Eating

Hoosier Mama Pie Company   PIES $

3 ✖ MAP P106, D7

Soothing 1950s pastels and antique pie tins set the Americana vibe at Paula Haney's celebrated pie shop, where hand-rolled, buttery-flaky crust is plumped full with fruit or creamy fillings. Favorites include sour-cream Dutch cranberry, banana cream, chocolate chess (aka 'brownie pie') and apple-blueberry-walnut. A handful of savory pies tempt, but let's not kid ourselves – we're here for the sweet stuff. (📞312-243-4846; www.hoosiermamapie.com; 1618 W Chicago Ave, East Village; slices

$5-6; ⊙8am-7pm Tue-Fri, 9am-5pm Sat, 10am-4pm Sun; 🚌66, Ⓜ Blue Line to Chicago)

Margie's Candies
DESSERTS $

4 ✘ MAP P106, A2

Margie's has held court at Bucktown's edge for more than 90 years, scooping ice-cream sundaes into giant clamshell bowls for everyone from Al Capone to the Beatles (check the wall photos). Admire the marble soda fountain and the booths with mini-jukeboxes, but the star is the hot fudge – unbelievably thick, rich and bountiful, and served in its own silver pot. (☎773-384-1035; www.margiesfinecandies.com; 1960 N Western Ave, Bucktown; sundaes from $6; ⊙9am-midnight Sun-Thu, to 1am Fri & Sat; 🚻; Ⓜ Blue Line to Western)

Irazu
LATIN AMERICAN $

5 ✘ MAP P106, A3

Chicago's lone Costa Rican hugely popular eatery turns out delicious burritos bursting with chicken, black beans and fresh avocado, and sandwiches dressed in a heavenly, spicy-sweet vegetable sauce. Wash them down with an *avena* (a slurpable milkshake in tropical-fruit flavors). For breakfast, the *arroz con huevos* (peppery eggs scrambled into rice) relieves hangovers. Speaking of which, Irazu is BYOB with no corkage fee. Cash only. (☎773-252-5687; www.irazuchicago. com; 1865 N Milwaukee Ave, Bucktown; mains $7-16; ⊙11:30am-9:30pm Mon-Sat; 🖋; Ⓜ Blue Line to Western)

Dove's Luncheonette (p110)

Dove's Luncheonette 🍽️

Sit at the retro counter of **Dove's Luncheonette** (Map p106, B4; 📞773-645-4060; www.doveschicago.com; 1545 N Damen Ave, Wicker Park; mains $13-22; 🕑9am-10pm Mon-Thu, to 11pm Fri, 8am-11pm Sat, 8am-10pm Sun; Ⓜ️Blue Line to Damen) for Tex-Mex plates of pork-shoulder posole and buttermilk fried chicken with chorizo-verde gravy. Soul music spins on a record player, tequila flows from the 70 bottles rattling behind the bar, and presto: all is right in the world.

Small Cheval   BURGERS $

6 ❌ MAP P106, B3

Maybe you've heard of Au Cheval, the foodie-adored West Loop joint with two-hour waits for its famed burgers, once crowned the nation's best by *Bon Appetit*? This pared-down kid sibling is a festive little shack serving up nothing but burgers. And boozy milkshakes, cocktails and beer. Wait time is minimal, and there's plenty of patio seating beneath the rumbling L. (www.smallcheval.com; 1732 N Milwaukee Ave, Wicker Park; burgers $9-10; 🕑11am-midnight Mon-Sat, to 10pm Sun; Ⓜ️Blue Line to Damen)

Big Star   MEXICAN $

7 ❌ MAP P106, B4

This former gas station is now a taco-serving honky-tonk bar from big-name Chicago chef Paul Kahan. The place gets packed but it's worth the wait – pork belly in tomato-*guajillo* chili sauce and mole-spiced carrots drizzled with date-infused yogurt accompany the whiskey- and agave-based cocktail list. Vegan options available. If the table-studded patio is too crowded, order from the walk-up window. (📞773-235-4039; www.bigstarchicago.com; 1531 N Damen Ave, Wicker Park; tacos $2.50-4; 🕑11:30am-1:30am Sun-Fri, to 3am Sat; 🚼; Ⓜ️Blue Line to Damen)

Handlebar   VEGETARIAN $

8 ❌ MAP P106, A4

The cult of the bike messenger runs strong in Chicago, and this clamorous restaurant-bar is a way station for tattooed couriers and locals who love the microbrew-centric beer list and the vegetarian/vegan comfort-food menu (which includes some fish dishes), such as West African ground-nut stew and fried avocado tacos. In summer head to the festive beer garden out back. (📞773-384-9546; www.handlebarchicago.com; 2311 W North Ave, Wicker Park; mains $10-14; 🕑10am-midnight Mon-Thu, to 12:30am Fri, 9am-12:30am Sat, 9am-midnight Sun; 🚼; Ⓜ️Blue Line to Damen)

Drinking

Violet Hour
COCKTAIL BAR

9 🚇 MAP P106, B4

This nouveau speakeasy isn't marked, so look for the wood-paneled building with a full mural and a yellow light over the door. Inside, high-backed booths, chandeliers and long velvet drapes provide the backdrop to elaborately engineered, award-winning seasonal cocktails with droll names. As highbrow as it sounds, friendly staff make Violet Hour welcoming and accessible. (📞773-252-1500; www.theviolethour.com; 1520 N Damen Ave, Wicker Park; ⏰6pm-2am Sun-Fri, to 3am Sat; Ⓜ Blue Line to Damen)

Matchbox
BAR

10 🚇 MAP P106, F7

Lawyers, artists and bums all squeeze in for retro cocktails. It's as small as – you got it – a matchbox, with about a dozen bar stools; everyone else stands against the back wall. Barkeeps make the drinks from scratch. Favorites include the pisco sour and the ginger gimlet, ladled from an amber vat of homemade ginger-infused vodka. (📞312-666-9292; www.facebook.com/matchboxchicago; 770 N Milwaukee Ave, River West; ⏰3pm-2am Sun-Fri, to 3am Sat; Ⓜ Blue Line to Chicago)

Innertown Pub
BAR

11 🚇 MAP P106, B6

A holiday-light-festooned moose head and a life-size statue of Elvis overlook the crowd of artsy regulars playing pool and drinking on the cheap at this lovably divey, kitsch-filled watering hole (and former 1920s speakeasy). The bartenders enjoy mixing up unconventional cocktails and DJs spin new wave and other tunes a few nights per week. (📞773-235-9795; 1935 W Thomas St, East Village; ⏰3pm-2am Sun-Fri, to 3am Sat; Ⓜ Blue Line to Division)

Rainbo Club
BAR

12 🚇 MAP P106, B5

The center for Chicago's indie elite during the week, the boxy, dark-wood 1930s Rainbo Club has an impressive semicircular bar and one of the city's best photo booths. The service is slow and the place goes a little suburban on weekends, but otherwise it's a fun spot to hang out with artsy locals quaffing $2 PBR drafts. Cash only. (📞773-489-5999; 1150 N Damen Ave, Ukrainian Village; ⏰4pm-2am Sun-Fri, to 3am Sat; Ⓜ Blue Line to Damen)

Entertainment

Hideout
LIVE MUSIC

13 ⭐ MAP P106, D3

Hidden behind a factory past the edge of Bucktown, this two-room lodge of indie rock and alt-country is well worth seeking out. The owners have nursed an outsider, underground vibe, and the place feels like your grandma's rumpus room. On Mondays there's a great open-mike **poetry night**. (www.facebook.com/weedspoetry; by donation; ⏰9:30pm)

Quimby's Bookstore

The epicenter of Chicago's comic and zine worlds, **Quimby's** (Map p106, C4; 773-342-0910; www.quimbys. com; 1854 W North Ave, Wicker Park; noon-9pm Mon-Thu, to 10pm Fri, 11am-10pm Sat, noon-7pm Sun; M Blue Line to Damen) is one of the linchpins of underground literary culture in the city. Here you can find everything from crayon-powered punk-rock manifestos to slickly produced graphic novels. It's a groovy place for cheeky literary souvenirs and bizarro readings.

Music and other events (talk shows, literary readings, comedy etc) take place nightly. (773-227-4433; www.hideoutchicago.com; 1354 W Wabansia Ave, West Town; tickets $5-15; 4pm-midnight Mon-Thu, to 2am Fri, 6pm-3am Sat, hours vary Sun; 72)

Empty Bottle   LIVE MUSIC

14 ⭐ MAP P106, A6

Chicago's music insiders fawn over the Empty Bottle, the city's scruffy, go-to club for edgy indie rock, jazz and other beats that's been a west-side institution for almost three decades. Monday's show is often a freebie by a couple of up-and-coming bands. Cheap beer, a photo booth and good graffiti-reading in the bathrooms add to the dive-bar fun.

(773-276-3600; www.emptybottle. com; 1035 N Western Ave, Ukrainian Village; 5pm-2am Mon-Wed, from 3pm Thu & Fri, from 11am Sat & Sun; 49)

House Theatre   THEATER

15 ⭐ MAP P106, D5

This exhilarating company presents a mix of quirky, funny, touching shows written by up-and-coming playwrights – magic, music and good old-fashioned storytelling usually tie in somehow. House typically performs at the on-site **Chopin Theatre** (773-278-1500; www.chopintheatre.com), but sometimes it turns up in offbeat locations (such as a hotel room) as well. The company also stages an annual ballet-free version of *The Nutcracker*. (773-769-3832; www.thehousetheatre.com; 1543 W Division St, Noble Square; M Blue Line to Division)

Shopping

Reckless Records   MUSIC

16 🔒 MAP P106, C4

Chicago's best indie-rock record and CD emporium lets you listen to everything before you buy. There's plenty of elbow room in the big, sunny space, which makes for happy hunting through the new and used bins. DVDs and cassette tapes, too. Stop by for flyers and listing calendars of the local live-music and theater scene. (773-235-3727; www. reckless.com; 1379 N Milwaukee Ave, Wicker Park; 10am-10pm Mon-Sat, to 8pm Sun; M Blue Line to Damen)

Dusty Groove

MUSIC

17 🛍 MAP P106, D5

Old-school soul, Latin beats, American gospel, bass-stabbing hip-hop, every flavor of jazz – if it's funky, Dusty Groove (which also has its own record label) stocks it. Flip through stacks of vinyl, or get lost amid the tidy shop's CDs. Be sure to check out the bargain basement, with boxes full of 50¢ records. (📞773-342-5800; www.dustygroove.com; 1120 N Ashland Ave, East Village; ⏱10am-8pm; Ⓜ Blue Line to Division)

Una Mae's

CLOTHING

18 🛍 MAP P106, C4

It's a fine spot to browse for a pillbox hat or a classic houndstooth-check jacket. Along with its vintage wares, Una Mae's has a collection of new, cool-cat designer duds, accessories and shoes for both men and women. (📞773-276-7002; www.unamaeschicago.com; 1528 N Milwaukee Ave, Wicker Park; ⏱noon-8pm Mon-Fri, from 11am Sat, noon-6pm Sun; Ⓜ Blue Line to Damen)

Transit Tees

GIFTS & SOUVENIRS

If you want to take a bit of Chi-town home with you, check out these locally made souvenirs with style (see **16** 🛍 Map p106, C4). Just about everything is emblazoned with the iconic two blue stripes and four red stars: throw pillows, socks, tumblers and, of course, T-shirts. There are also transit maps, Chicago posters and street signs. (www.transittees.com; 1371 N Milwaukee Ave, Wicker Park; ⏱9:30am-8pm Mon-Fri, from 11am Sat, 11am-6pm Sun)

Reckless Records

Wicker Park, Bucktown & Ukrainian Village Shopping

Worth a Trip 🥾

A Night Out
in Logan Square

Logan Square is the 'it' neighborhood for new and cool. But it's also refreshingly low-key, since it's somewhat off the beaten path. Art displays, Beard Award–winning kitchens and dive bars chock-full of local color dot the leafy boulevards. Try to arrive early in the evening to take advantage of the shops and galleries.

Walk Facts

Start Whistler (Ⓜ Blue Line to California)

End Lost Lake (Ⓜ Blue Line to Logan Square)

Length 1.5 miles; four to five hours

❶ Whistler

Whistler (📞773-227-3530; www.
whistlerchicago.com; 2421 N Milwaukee Ave; ⏰6pm-2am Mon-Thu, 5pm-
2am Fri-Sun) is part art gallery and
part venue for local indie bands,
jazz combos and DJs. No cover
charge, but buy a snazzy cocktail
to fund the performances.

❷ Heavy Feather

Heavy Feather(📞773-799-8504;
www.heavyfeatherchicago.com; 2357
N Milwaukee Ave; ⏰7pm-2am Sun-Fri,
to 3am Sat) was modeled after fern
bars of the late 1970s and early
'80s – plant-adorned drinking
establishments replete with wood
accents and faux Tiffany lamps.
The cocktail bar is a darkly lit
hideaway located above the bar
Slippery Slope. The drinks are
modern takes on classics, such as
the chai toddy with cognac,
applejack and spicy tea.

❸ Cole's

Head to dimly lit dive bar **Cole's**
(📞773-276-5802; www.coleschicago.
com; 2338 N Milwaukee Ave; ⏰5pm-
2am Mon-Fri, 4pm-3am Sat, 4pm-2am
Sun) to play pool and suck down
microbrews in the neon-bathed
front room, and to listen to bands
and open-mike comedy in the
back room.

❹ Revolution Brewing

Revolution (📞773-227-2739; www.
revbrew.com; 2323 N Milwaukee Ave;
⏰11am-1am Mon-Fri, 10am-1am Sat,
10am-11pm Sun) was one of the
first breweries on the scene here.
The strong beers kick butt, like
the Anti-Hero IPA and Freedom of
Press sour. Order the bacon-fat
popcorn with fried sage to steady
yourself.

❺ Pretty Cool Ice Cream

There's something for everyone at
Pretty Cool Ice Cream (📞773-
697-4140; www.prettycoolicecream.
com; 2353 N California Ave; ice-cream
bars $3-5; ⏰11am-11pm May-Sep,
reduced hours Oct-Apr; 🖉), with addictive flavors like strawberry but-
termilk, coffee pretzel toffee and
matcha mint. No scoops though
– all treats come on a stick.

❻ Fat Rice

Tiny **Fat Rice** (📞773-661-9170;
www.eatfatrice.com; 2957 W Diversey
Ave; mains $20-32; ⏰5:30-10pm
Tue, 11am-2pm & 5:30-10pm Wed-
Sat, 11am-3pm Sun), purveyor
of Macanese cuisine, is crazy
popular, especially since the chef
won a 2018 James Beard Award.
Book ahead to chow on the
Portuguese-Chinese-Indian food
mash-up.

❼ Lost Lake

Lost Lake (📞773-293-6048; www.
lostlaketiki.com; 3154 W Diversey Ave;
⏰5pm-2am Mon-Fri, 4pm-3am Sat,
4pm-2am Sun) recreates a flawless
South Seas vibe. The bamboo decor, insane collection of rum and
nationally acclaimed cocktails
made with exotic ingredients are
pure magic.

Explore ◈
West Loop &
Near West Side

Edgy West Loop buzzes with hot-chef restaurants and on-trend bars that have taken over former meatpacking factories. Development continues big-time, with condos, tech company offices and the hippest brand hotels rising at a dizzying pace. Eating and drinking here is an essential. Greektown and Little Italy are nearby and also fun for a night out.

The Short List

○ **Starry food (p124)** Forking into a decadent meal by a celebrity chef at one of the mega-hot restaurants in the district, like Stephanie Izard's Girl & the Goat.

○ **Fancy cocktails (p126)** Swirling a magical drink at the champagne bars, rooftop bars and distilleries such as exemplary Aviary.

○ **Greektown (p123)** Exploring the tavernas, bakeries and shops along Halsted St and indulging in flaming cheese and honeyed sweets; Artopolis shows how it's done.

○ **Carrie Secrist Gallery (p122)** Wandering around the old warehouses to find art hubs such as this contemporary haven.

Getting There & Around

Ⓜ Green, Pink Lines to Morgan or Clinton for West Loop; Blue Line to UIC-Halsted for Greektown; Pink Line to Polk or Blue Line to Racine for Little Italy.

🚌 The West Loop and Greektown are only 1.25 miles west of the Loop, making them a fairly cheap ride.

Neighborhood Map on p120

Mexican restaurant in Little Italy, Near West Side
TODD BANNOR/ALAMY STOCK PHOTO ©

Walking Tour 🥾

West Loop Wander

West Loop has exploded in recent years with hotshot restaurants and condos carved from old meatpacking warehouses. While a few bloody-apron-clad workers remain, these days you're more likely to run into a Google employee toting a latte as you traverse the galleries and mega-stylish eateries inhabiting the industrial buildings.

Walk Facts

Start Saint Lou's Assembly (Ⓜ️ Green, Pink Line to Clinton)

End Smyth (Ⓜ️ Green, Pink Line to Ashland)

Length 1.25 miles; four to five hours

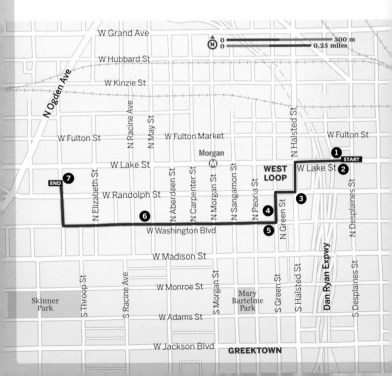

❶ Saint Lou's Assembly

Saint Lou's Assembly (p124) draws a crowd for its 'meat and three' meals. The concept harks back to West Loop's factory past, when cafeterias served the combination to workers. Lou's offers a modern version of the meat main and three side dishes, along with cocktails and a rollicking patio with a boccie court.

❷ Open Books

Thrifty hipsters in need of a good read browse the gently used stacks at **Open Books** (p127). Hours slip by as they scan shelves that hold *Little House on the Prairie* next to Gwyneth Paltrow's latest cookbook next to a 1987 guidebook to Alaska. All proceeds go toward the nonprofit shop's literacy programs for local kids.

❸ Haymarket Pub & Brewery

Haymarket Pub & Brewery (p127) provides a nice dose of local history. It's located near where the 1886 Haymarket labor riot took place, and the brewery's suds often have affiliated names, such as the Mathias Imperial IPA (named after the first police officer to die in the melee) and the Speakerswagon Pilsner.

❹ Sawada Coffee

West Loop workers at Google, Uber and the district's other tech companies need to stay caffeinated, and **Sawada Coffee** (☎ 312-754-0431; www.sawadacoffee.com; 112 N Green St, West Loop; ◷ 8am-5pm; ☎) provides the requisite lattes. The signature one is made with matcha (green tea powder) and poured exquisitely. Sawada's wi-fi, epicurean doughnuts and rustic-chic interior invite lingering.

❺ Carrie Secrist Gallery

See what's showing at **Carrie Secrist Gallery** (p122). She has been organizing heady exhibitions of contemporary works for more than 25 years. Three other galleries share the building, so you can really dive into the local art scene.

❻ Press Room

Follow the green neon 'Down for a Drink' sign to the **Press Room** (p127). The European-style wine bar is a convivial gathering spot for neighborhood dwellers. Join them for a glass of cava and plate of Spanish anchovies. It's located in the basement of a century-old publishing house, hence the name.

❼ Smyth

It's totally worth it to reserve ahead and sink your teeth into the Michelin-starred tasting menu at **Smyth** (p125). But you have options if you don't get in. Smyth's sister restaurant the Loyalist sits in the basement, a neighborhood favorite for its mighty cheeseburger and rich desserts.

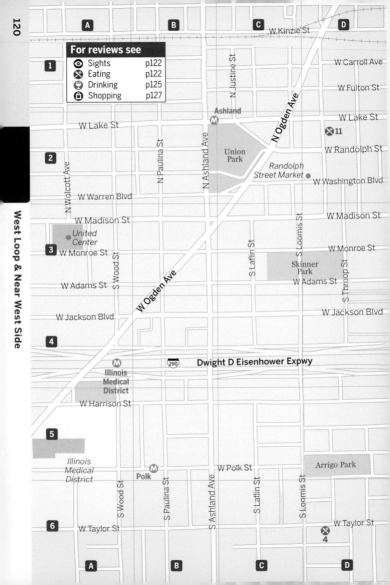

West Loop & Near West Side

For reviews see

⊙ Sights	p122
⊗ Eating	p122
🍷 Drinking	p125
🔒 Shopping	p127

A B C D

1

2

3

4

5

6

W Kinzie St

W Carroll Ave

W Fulton St

N Ogden Ave

Ashland Ⓜ

W Lake St

⊗ 11

W Lake St

Union Park

W Randolph St

N Justine St

N Paulina St

N Ashland Ave

Randolph Street Market ●

W Washington Blvd

N Wolcott Ave

W Warren Blvd

W Madison St

W Madison St

United Center ●

S Loomis St

W Monroe St

W Monroe St

S Wood St

Skinner Park

W Adams St

S Laflin St

S Throop St

W Adams St

W Jackson Blvd

W Ogden Ave

W Jackson Blvd

Ⓜ Illinois Medical District

290 Dwight D Eisenhower Expwy

W Harrison St

Illinois Medical District

S Wood St

S Paulina St

Ⓜ Polk

W Polk St

S Ashland Ave

Arrigo Park

S Laflin St

S Loomis St

W Taylor St

⊗ 4

W Taylor St

A B C D

E

F

G

H

W Kinzie St

0 500 m
0 0.25 miles

1

14

W Fulton Market

W Fulton St

Mars
2 Gallery

Morgan

15

WEST
LOOP

3

Clinton

9

W Lake St

8

18

12

13

10

17

W Randolph St

6

2

N Racine Ave

N May St

N Carpenter St

N Sangamon St

N Peoria St

N Halsted St

N Green St

16

7

Carrie Secrist
Gallery 1

W Washington St

W Madison St

Chicago-Ogilvie
Transportation
Center (Metra)

S Racine Ave

S Aberdeen St

S Morgan St

Mary
Bartelme
Park

W Monroe St

3

W Adams St

Chicago-
Union Station
(Metra)

GREEKTOWN

S Peoria St

S Halsted St

W Jackson Blvd

Lou
Mitchell's

5

W Van Buren St

W Van Buren St

4

Racine

UIC-Halsted

Clinton

W Harrison St

S Jefferson St

S Clinton St

5

S Racine Ave

W Polk St
W Cabrini St

S May St

S Morgan St

University
of Illinois
at Chicago

S Halsted St

S Desplaines St

LITTLE
ITALY

W Taylor St

6

E

F

G

H

Sights

Carrie Secrist Gallery GALLERY

1 MAP P120, F2

Secrist's contemporary gallery has been around for more than a quarter century. The big, open space hosts about six different exhibitions per year, both solo and group shows of provocative painters, photographers, filmmakers and artists working in other mediums. It's one of West Loop's coolest galleries. The building is also home to three other galleries. (312-491-0917; www.secristgallery.com; 835 W Washington Blvd, 1st fl, West Loop; ⏱10:30am-6pm Tue-Fri, 11am-5pm Sat; Ⓜ Green, Pink Line to Morgan)

Mars Gallery GALLERY

2 MAP P120, E1

This pop-art gallery is pure fun, from the colorful, cartoony prints and paintings to the building's offbeat history (it was an egg factory and then a club where the Ramones played). Weird bonus: it sits atop an energy vortex. (312-226-7808; www.marsgallery.com; 1139 W Fulton Market, West Loop; ⏱noon-6pm Wed & Fri, to 7pm Thu, 11am-5pm Sat; Ⓜ Green, Pink Line to Morgan)

Eating

Publican Quality Meats DELI $

3 MAP P120, F1

This butcher shop and 32-seat eatery is the casual, cheaper sibling to nearby **Publican** (312-733-9555; 837 W Fulton Market; mains $21-30; ⏱3:30-10pm Mon-Thu, to 11pm Fri, 10am-11pm Sat, 9am-10pm Sun). Grab a seat at a table in back and bite into a sandwich of delicately cured meat on just-baked bread. The lineup changes weekly, but might include the beefy meatball sandwich or thick-cut bacon, lettuce and tomato on sourdough. Also a tidy beer and wine list. (312-445-8977; www.thepublicanrestaurant.com; 825 W Fulton Market, West Loop; mains $11-14; ⏱10am-5pm Mon-Fri, 9am-6pm Sat, 9am-5pm Sun; Ⓜ Green, Pink Line to Morgan)

Sweet Maple Cafe AMERICAN $

4 MAP P120, D6

The creaking floorboards, matronly staff and soulful home cookin' lend the Sweet Maple Cafe the bucolic appeal of a Southern roadside diner. The signature dishes – inch-thick banana (or, seasonally, peaches and cream)

West Loop Street Art

Check out the B_Line (www.blinechicago.com), a mile-long street art corridor that stretches along W Hubbard St between Halsted and Carpenter Sts. More than three dozen murals decorate the walls that flank the Metra train tracks here, including a sweet one of DJ Frankie Knuckles (the local who popularized house music).

pancakes, cheddar grits and fluffy biscuits that come smothered in spicy sausage gravy – earn the superlatives of locals. (☎ 312-243-8908; www.sweetmaplecafe.com; 1339 W Taylor St, Little Italy; mains $10-14; ⏱7am-2pm; Ⓜ Blue Line to Racine)

Artopolis Bakery & Cafe
GREEK $

5 ✖ MAP P120, G4

Artopolis is one of the city's top bakeries – many of the nearby Randolph St restaurants get their bread here, and locals often pop in to ogle the pastries glistening in the cases. It's also a cafe-bar that opens onto the street, with wine-laden tables along the front. Wood-fired pizzas, spinach-and-feta pies and roasted chicken top the menu. (☎ 312-559-9000; www.artopolischicago.com; 306 S Halsted St, Greektown; mains $10-18; ⏱8:30am-11pm Sun-Thu, to 12:30am Fri & Sat; Ⓜ Blue Line to UIC-Halsted)

Avec
MEDITERRANEAN $$

6 ✖ MAP P120, H2

Feeling social? This happening spot gives diners a chance to rub elbows at eight-person communal tables. The mini room looks like a Finnish sauna and fills with noisy chatter as stylish urbanites pile in. The bacon-wrapped dates are the menu's must-try; the tasty paella and the sausage and mint-pesto calzone are other stand-outs, though the menu changes regularly. Reservations are a good idea, but they're only taken during

Chicago Hockey & Basketball

The busy **United Center** (Map p120, A3; ☎ 312-455-4500; www.unitedcenter.com; 1901 W Madison St, Near West Side; 🚌19, 20) is Chicago's arena for big-name concerts and sporting events. The pro-hockey team the Blackhawks (www.nhl.com/blackhawks) and pro-basketball team the Bulls (www.nba.com/bulls) both play here from October through April. The slam-dunking Michael Jordan statue is a famed photo op; it's in the glass atrium on the building's eastern side.

off-peak hours. (☎ 312-377-2002; www.avecrestaurant.com; 615 W Randolph St, West Loop; mains $18-28; ⏱11:30am-2pm & 3:30-11pm Mon-Thu, 11:30am-2pm & 3:30pm-midnight Fri, 3:30pm-midnight Sat, 10am-2pm & 3:30-11pm Sun; Ⓜ Green, Pink Line to Clinton)

Monteverde
ITALIAN $$

7 ✖ MAP P120, E3

Housemade pastas are the specialty here. They seem simple in concept, such as the *cacio whey pepe* (small tube pasta with pecorino Romano, ricotta whey and four-peppercorn blend), but the flavors are lusciously complex. That's why the light-wood tables in the lively room are always packed. Reserve ahead, especially for weekends, or try the bar or patio

Lou Mitchell's 🍴

A relic of Route 66, **Lou Mitchell's** (Map p120, H4; 📞312-939-3111; www.loumitchells.com; 565 W Jackson Blvd, West Loop; mains $9-14; ⏰5:30am-3pm Mon, to 4pm Tue-Fri, 7am-4pm Sat, to 3pm Sun; 👶; Ⓜ Blue Line to Clinton) brings in elbow-to-elbow locals and tourists for breakfast. Old-school waitstaff deliver big fluffy omelets and thick-cut French toast with a jug of syrup. They call you 'honey' and fill your coffee cup endlessly. There's often a queue to get in, but free doughnut holes and Milk Duds help ease the wait.

for walk-in seats. (📞312-888-3041; www.monteverdechicago.com; 1020 W Madison St, West Loop; mains $18-24; ⏰5-10:30pm Tue-Fri, 11:30am-10:30pm Sat, 11:30am-9pm Sun; Ⓜ Green, Pink Line to Morgan)

Au Cheval AMERICAN $$

8 🍴 MAP P120, G2

People go crazy over Au Cheval's cheeseburger. It drips with a runny fried egg, melty cheddar and tangy dijonnaise, all stuffed into a super-fluffy bun. *Bon Appetit* crowned it America's best burger, and the little diner has been mobbed since. No reservations, so prepare to wait (best done at the neighboring bar; staff will text when your table is ready). (📞312-929-4580; www.

auchevalchicago.com; 800 W Randolph St, West Loop; mains $13-19; ⏰10am-1am Mon-Sat, 9am-midnight Sun; Ⓜ Green, Pink Line to Morgan)

Saint Lou's Assembly AMERICAN $$

9 🍴 MAP P120, G1

Casual Lou's pays homage to the area's meatpacking past, when 'meat and three' cafeterias – where you'd select a meaty main dish and three sides – were popular. This is the modern version, so take a seat in a retro blue-vinyl booth and choose among Peruvian-style chicken, chili-marinated sirloin steak, kimchi and collard greens, and other modern takes on nostalgic fare. (📞312-600-0600; www.saintlouschicago.com; 664 W Lake St, West Loop; mains $16-20; ⏰11am-3pm & 5pm-midnight Mon-Thu, to 2am Fri, 9am-2am Sat, 9am-midnight Sun; Ⓜ Green, Pink Line to Clinton)

Girl & the Goat AMERICAN $$$

10 🍴 MAP P120, G2

Stephanie Izard's flagship restaurant rocks. The soaring ceilings, polished wood tables and cartoony art on the walls offer a convivial atmosphere where local beer and housemade wine hit the tables, along with unique small plates such as catfish with pickled persimmons. Reservations are difficult; try for walk-in seats before 5pm or see if anything opens up at the bar. (📞312-492-6262; www.girlandthegoat.com; 809 W Randolph St, West Loop; small plates $12-19; ⏱4:30-11pm Sun-Thu, to midnight Fri & Sat; 🍴; Ⓜ Green, Pink Line to Morgan)

Smyth

AMERICAN $$$

11 🍴 MAP P120, D2

Smyth is a homey spot that's bagged a pair of Michelin stars for its seasonal tasting menus. Prepare to spend two to three hours making your way through five to 12 courses of elevated comfort food, say biscuits with ramp honey or lamb with juniper. Ingredients come from Smyth's partner farm, located about an hour south of the city. Reservations required. (📞773-913-3773; www.smythandtheloyalist.com; 177 N Ada St, West Loop; tasting menus $95-225; ⏱5-10pm Tue-Sat; Ⓜ Green, Pink Line to Ashland)

Drinking

CH Distillery

DISTILLERY

12 🍷 MAP P120, H2

This slick tasting room has a cool, naturalistic look with exposed concrete posts and knotty wood beams across the ceiling. Slip into a seat at the bar and watch the silver tanks behind the big glass window distilling the organic vodka and gin that go into your creative cocktail. (📞312-707-8780; www.chdistillery.com; 564 W Randolph St, West Loop; ⏱4-10pm Mon-Thu, to midnight Fri & Sat; Ⓜ Green, Pink Line to Clinton)

Girl & the Goat

RM Champagne Salon WINE BAR

13 🚇 MAP P120, F2

This West Loop spot is a twinkling-light charmer for bubbles. Score a table in the cobblestoned courtyard and you'll feel transported to Paris. In winter, the indoor fireplace and plush seats provide a toasty refuge. (📞312-243-1199; www.rmchampagnesalon.com; 116 N Green St, West Loop; ⏰5pm-midnight Mon-Wed & Sun, 5pm-2am Thu-Sat, plus 11am-2pm Sat & Sun; Ⓜ Green, Pink Line to Morgan)

Waydown ROOFTOP BAR

14 🚇 MAP P120, F1

The Ace Hotel's rooftop bar wins praise for several reasons. It provides terrific skyline views. It draws a superstylish crowd, but there's no velvet rope attitude. And it makes lovely cocktails with seasonal juices, vermouths and mezcals that aren't that pricey considering the neighborhood. Bands or DJs provide the soundtrack most nights. (📞312-764-1919; www.acehotel.com; 311 N Morgan St, 7th fl, West Loop; ⏰4pm-2am Mon-Fri, from 3pm Sat & Sun; Ⓜ Green, Pink Line to Morgan)

Aviary COCKTAIL BAR

15 🚇 MAP P120, F1

The Aviary is a James Beard Award winner for best cocktails in the nation. The ethereal drinks are like nothing you've laid lips on before. Some arrive with Bunsen burners, others with a slingshot you use to break the ice. They taste terrific, whatever the science involved. It's

West Fulton Market streetscape

wise to make reservations online. Drinks range between $21 and $29 each. (www.theaviary.com; 955 W Fulton Market, West Loop; ⏰5pm-midnight Sun-Wed, to 2am Thu-Sat; MGreen, Pink Line to Morgan)

Press Room
WINE BAR

16 🚇 MAP P120, E2

Groups of friends and couples on dates descend to the Press Room's snug basement digs to chitchat at candlelit tables over glasses of red, white and sparkling wines. More than 20 are available by the glass, along with a small cocktail and beer menu. The tranquil vibe is unusual – and much appreciated – in buzzing West Loop. (📞331-240-1914; www.pressroomchicago.com; 1134 W Washington Blvd, West Loop; ⏰4pm-midnight Mon-Sat; MGreen, Pink Line to Morgan)

Haymarket Pub & Brewery
BREWERY

17 🚇 MAP P120, G2

An early arrival on the West Loop scene, Haymarket remains nicely low-key. It doesn't try to win you over with uberhipness like many of its neighbors. Locals hang out in the cavernous, barrel-strewn space drinking fresh-from-the-tank recipes. The focus is on classic Belgian and German styles, but saisons, IPAs and barrel-aged barley wines fill glasses, too. (📞312-638-0700; www.haymarketbeer.com; 737 W Randolph St, West Loop; ⏰11am-2am Sun-Fri, to 3am Sat; MGreen, Pink Line to Clinton)

Randolph Street Market

This **market** (Map p120, D2; 📞312-666-1200; www.randolphstreetmarket.com; 1340 W Washington Blvd, West Loop; $10-12; ⏰10am-5pm last weekend of month Feb-Dec; MGreen, Pink Line to Ashland), which styles itself on London's Portobello Market, has become quite the to-do in town. It takes place inside the beaux-arts Plumbers Hall, where more than 200 antique dealers hock collectibles, costume jewelry, furniture, books, Turkish rugs and pinball machines.

Shopping

Open Books
BOOKS

18 🔒 MAP P120, G2

Buy a used book here and you're helping to fund this volunteer-based literacy group's programs, which range from in-school reading help for grade-schoolers to book-publishing courses for teens. The jam-packed store has good-quality tomes and plenty of cushy sofas where you can sit and peruse your finds. Kids will find lots of imaginative wares. Books average around $5. (📞312-475-1355; www.open-books.org; 651 W Lake St, West Loop; ⏰9am-7pm Mon-Sat, noon-6pm Sun; ♿; MGreen, Pink Line to Clinton)

Explore 🧭
Pilsen &
Near South Side

This area spans a huge range of things to do. The Field Museum, Shedd Aquarium and Adler Planetarium cluster at the lakefront Museum Campus; nearby are historic house museums and a famed blues sight. At the southern edge, Chinatown bustles with noodle shops and exotic wares. Further west is Pilsen, where Mexican culture mixes with Chicago's bohemian underground.

The Short List

○ **Field Museum of Natural History (p130)** *Sizing up Sue the T rex at one of the world's foremost scientific research institutions.*

○ **National Museum of Mexican Art (p136)** *Admiring colorful folk art at the USA's largest Latinx arts institution.*

○ **Chinatown (p139)** *Nibbling almond cookies in the bakeries and shopping for trinkets in the shops.*

○ **Northerly Island (p136)** *Walking or cycling around the wild, grassy island and checking out the birdlife en route.*

Getting There & Around

🚌 Numbers 130 (in summer) and 146 (year-round) go to the Museum Campus.

Ⓜ Red, Orange, Green Line to Roosevelt for Museum Campus. Red Line to Cermak-Chinatown for Chinatown. Green Line to Cermak-McCormick Pl for McCormick Place.

🚗 The Museum Campus boasts plenty of lot parking (from $19 per car on non-event days).

Neighborhood Map on p134

Top Sight 📷
Field Museum of Natural History

The mammoth Field Museum houses everything but the kitchen sink. The collection's rock star is Sue, the largest Tyrannosaurus rex yet discovered. She's 13ft tall and 41ft long, and menaces the 2nd floor with ferocious aplomb. The galleries beyond hold 30 million other artifacts, tended by a slew of PhD-wielding scientists, as the Field remains an active research institution.

◉ MAP P134, E2

📞 312-922-9410

www.fieldmuseum.org

1400 S Lake Shore Dr, Near South Side; adult/child $24/17; ⊙ 9am-5pm

🚌 146, 130

Dinosaur Stash

The first dinosaur you'll encounter is a plant-eating titanosaur named Maximo, who rules over the main floor. He's even bigger than Sue. He's a cast (not real bones), so feel free to touch him. After communing with Max, dino lovers should head up to the **Evolving Planet** exhibit on the 2nd floor, which has more of the big guys and gals. This is where Sue lives in a private suite with accompanying videos that show what life was like for her back in the day. You can learn about the evolution of various species and watch staff paleontologists clean up fossils in the lab.

Mummies Galore

Inside Ancient Egypt re-creates an Egyptian burial chamber on two levels. The mastaba (tomb) contains 23 actual mummies and is a reconstruction of the one built for Unis-ankh, the son of the last pharaoh of the Fifth dynasty, who died at age 21 in 2407 BC. The relic-strewn bottom level is especially worthwhile.

Gems & Stuffed Animals

Other displays that merit your time include the **Hall of Gems** and its glittering garnets, opals, emeralds, pearls and diamonds. The Northwest Coast and Arctic Peoples' **totem-pole collection** got its start with artifacts shipped to Chicago for the 1893 World's Expo. And the largest man-eating lion ever caught is stuffed and standing sentry on the basement floor. Preserved insects and birds, and Bush-man, the cantankerous ape who drew crowds at Lincoln Park Zoo for decades, are also on display in all their taxidermic glory.

★ Top Tips

o Ask for the 'Basic' admission to see everything mentioned here.

o The 'All Access' and 'Discovery' admission tickets include extras such as the 3-D movie and special exhibits, which can be too much if you're doing lots of sightseeing.

o The shops inside are worth a browse for their abundant dino gear and educational toys.

✕ Take a Break

Relax in the beer garden and chomp into tavern-style pizza at **Flo & Santos** (☑312-566-9817; www.floandsantos.com; 1310 S Wabash Ave, Near South Side; mains $12-19; ⏱11:30am-11pm Sun-Thu, to midnight Fri & Sat; Ⓜ Red, Orange, Green Line to Roosevelt).

Hot dog and snack vendors set up around the museum on the lake side. Or you can walk over to the taco bar on 12th Street Beach (p137).

Walking Tour 🚶

Pilsen Old & New

Pilsen mixes it up. On one hand it's a center of Mexican culture, with paleta (popsicle) shops, taquerias and Virgin of Guadalupe murals. On the other hand it's a hipster district, with vintage shops, juice bars and brewpubs. Before either of these cultures arrived, Pilsen was home to Czech immigrants who named the area after a city in their homeland. You'll see it all as you walk through the neighborhood.

Walk Facts

Start 18th Street L station (Pink Line)

End 18th Street L station

Length 2 miles; two hours

❶ 18th Street L

Start at the **18th Street L station**. Murals cover every inch of the walls and stairs. Aztec gods and skeletons predominate.

❷ National Museum of Mexican Art

Walk west on 18th St to Wood St and turn south, skirting the park. At 19th St turn west to reach the **National Museum of Mexican Art** (p136). The vibrant collection of paintings and folk art is awesome and free.

❸ Gulliver in Wonderland

Return to 19th St heading west, and turn south onto Wolcott Ave. In one block you'll arrive at the home of muralist Hector Duarte, who has covered the exterior with **Gulliver in Wonderland** (1900 W Cullerton St), which shows a Mexican immigrant trying to break free from barbed wire.

❹ Alulu Brewery & Pub

Head east on Cullerton St for four blocks to Laflin St, and turn south. Mosey over to **Alulu Brewery & Pub** (📞312-600-9865; www.alulubrew.com; 2011 S Laflin St; ⏱5pm-2am Mon, Wed & Thu, 3pm-2am Fri & Sun, 3pm-3am Sat), an

intimate hangout for Pilsen's young and stylish. Housemade suds and pub grub like beer cheese curds keep the place buzzing.

❺ La Michoacana Premium

It's a whole different scene a few blocks northeast on Blue Island Ave at **La Michoacana Premium** (📞312-226-9600; www.lamichoacanapremiumpilsen.com; 1855 S Blue Island Ave; popsicles & ice-cream scoops $2-5.50; ⏱7am-11pm Mon-Thu, to midnight Fri-Sun), a pink ice-creamshop palace of gorgeous, fruit-studded *paletas*.

❻ Thalia Hall

Within a few blocks you'll arrive at **Thalia Hall** (p140), an 1892 building patterned after Prague's opera house. Today it hosts rock bands.

❼ Allport St Embankment

Head north on Allport St for a block until it dead-ends at the **train embankment**. This is a huge alfresco gallery for street art. Turn west on 16th St and follow the murals for three-quarters of a mile. At Wood St turn south, walk two blocks to 18th St, and head east. See the train station? You've just looped your way through Pilsen.

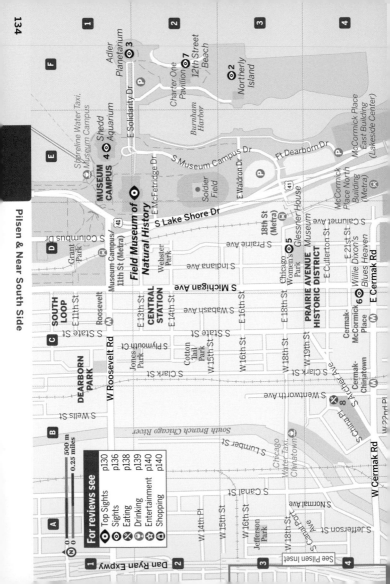

Pilsen & Near South Side

For reviews see
◆ Top Sights   p130
⊙ Sights   p136
⊗ Eating   p138
⊗ Drinking   p139
⊗ Entertainment   p140
⊗ Shopping   p140

500 m
0.25 miles

Dan Ryan Expwy

SOUTH LOOP

DEARBORN PARK

CENTRAL STATION

South Branch Chicago River

Chicago Water Taxi, Chinatown

Chinatown

W Cermak Rd

See Pilsen inset

Grant Park

Museum Campus/
11th St (Metra)

MUSEUM CAMPUS

Shoreline Water Taxi,
Museum Campus

Adler Planetarium ⊙3

Charter One Pavilion ⊙7
12th Street Beach

Burnham Harbor

Northerly Island ⊙2

Shedd Aquarium ⊙4

E Solidarity Dr

Field Museum of
Natural History ◆

S Lake Shore Dr

E McFridge Dr

Soldier Field

E Waldron Dr

Ft Dearborn Dr

S Museum Campus Dr

McCormick Place
East Building
(Lakeside Center)

McCormick
Place North
Building
(Metra)

Glessner House

Chicago Women's Park ⊙5

18th St (Metra)

S Prairie Ave

S Indiana Ave

S Michigan Ave

Webster Park

Roosevelt

W Roosevelt Rd

E 11th St

E 13th St

E 14th St

Cotton Tail Park

Jones Park

S Plymouth Ct

S Clark St

S State St

S Wabash Ave

S Wells St

W 14th Pl

W 15th St

W 16th St

S Canal St

Lumber St

PRAIRIE AVENUE
HISTORIC DISTRICT

E Cullerton St

E 21st St

S Calumet Ave

Willie Dixon's
Blues Heaven ⊙6

Cermak-
McCormick
Place

E Cermak Rd

Cermak-
Chinatown

S Archer Ave

S China Pl

W 22nd Pl

S Wentworth Ave

S Canal Port Ave

S Normal Ave

S Jefferson St

W 18th St

W 16th St

W 15th St

⊗8

Pilsen & Near South Side

Pilsen & Near South Side

Sights

National Museum of Mexican Art

MUSEUM

1 ⦿ MAP P134, A7

Founded in 1982, this vibrant museum – the largest Latinx arts institution in the US – has become one of the city's best. The vivid permanent collection sums up 1000 years of Mexican art and culture through classical paintings, shining gold altars, skeleton-rich folk art, beadwork and much more. (📞312-738-1503; www.national museumofmexicanart.org; 1852 W 19th St, Pilsen; admission free; ⏰10am-5pm Tue-Sun; Ⓜ Pink Line to 18th St)

Northerly Island

PARK

2 ⦿ MAP P134, F3

This hilly, prairie-grassed park has a walking and cycling trail, bird-watching, fishing and an outdoor venue for big-name concerts. It's actually a peninsula, not an island, but the Chicago skyline views are tremendous no matter what you call it. Stop in at the field house, if it's open, for tour information. Bicycles are available at the Divvy bike-share station by the Adler Planetarium. Note that parts of the trail are closed at times due to weather damage. (1521 S Linn White Dr, Near South Side; 🚌146, 130)

Adler Planetarium

MUSEUM

3 ⦿ MAP P134, F1

Space enthusiasts will get a big bang (pun!) out of the Adler. There are public telescopes to view the stars (10am to 1pm daily, by the Galileo Cafe), 3-D lectures to learn about supernovas (in the **Space Visualization Lab**), and the **Planet Explorers** exhibit where kids can 'launch' a rocket. The immersive digital films cost extra (from $13 per ticket). The Adler's front steps offer Chicago's best skyline view, so get your camera ready. (📞312-922-7827; www.adlerplanetarium.org; 1300 S Lake Shore Dr, Near South Side; adult/child $12/8; ⏰9:30am-4pm; 🚻; 🚌146, 130)

Shedd Aquarium

AQUARIUM

4 ⦿ MAP P134, E1

Top draws at the kiddie-mobbed Shedd Aquarium include the **Wild Reef** exhibit, where there's just 5in of Plexiglas between you and two-dozen fierce-looking sharks, and the **Oceanarium**, with its rescued sea otters. Note the Oceanarium also keeps beluga whales and Pacific white-sided dolphins, a practice that's increasingly frowned upon as captivity is stressful for these sensitive creatures. (📞312-939-2438; www.sheddaquarium.org; 1200 S Lake Shore Dr, Near South Side; adult/child $40/30; ⏰9am-6pm Jun-Aug, 9am-5pm Mon-Fri, to 6pm Sat & Sun Sep-May; 🚻; 🚌146, 130)

Glessner House Museum

MUSEUM

5 ⦿ MAP P134, D3

The 1887 John J Glessner House is the premier survivor of the **Prairie Avenue Historic District**. Much of the interior is reminiscent of an English manor house, with heavy wooden beams and other English-style details. Additionally, more than 80% of the current furnishings are authentic, thanks to the Glessner family's penchant for family photos. Tours (75 minutes) take it all in. (📞312-326-1480; www.glessnerhouse.org; 1800 S Prairie Ave, Near South Side; tours adult/child $15/8, admission Wed free; ⏱tours 11:30am, 1pm & 2:30pm Wed-Sun; 🚌1)

Willie Dixon's Blues Heaven
HISTORIC BUILDING

6 ◎ MAP P134, C4

From 1957 to 1967, this humble building was Chess Records, the seminal electric blues label. It's now named for the bassist who wrote most of Chess' hits. Staff give hour-long tours of the premises. It's pretty ramshackle, with few original artifacts on display. Still, hard-core fans will get a thrill out of hearing stories from the heady era and walking into the studio where their musical heroes recorded. Free blues concerts rock the side garden on summer Thursdays at 6pm. (📞312-808-1286; www.bluesheaven.com; 2120 S Michigan Ave, Near South Side; adult/child $15/10; ⏱noon-4pm Tue-Sat; Ⓜ Green Line to Cermak-McCormick Place)

12th Street Beach
BEACH

7 ◎ MAP P134, F2

A path runs south from the Adler Planetarium to this crescent of sand. Despite its proximity to the visitor-mobbed Museum Campus,

Shedd Aquarium

Pilsen Public Art Tours

Murals are a traditional Mexican art form, and they're splashed all over Pilsen's buildings. Local artists and activists lead these highly recommended **walking tours** (☏773-787-6847; www.ppat.space; 1hr tours per group $125) that take in the neighborhood's most impressive works. Call or go online to arrange an excursion (including meeting place and time).

the small beach remains bizarrely (but happily) secluded. There aren't many amenities besides a bathhouse, a taco shop and a couple of picnic tables. (www.cpdbeaches.com; 1200 S Linn White Dr, Near South Side; ⏱6am-11pm; ☒146, 130)

Eating

Qing Xiang Yuan Dumplings

DUMPLINGS $

8 ✖ MAP P134, B4

The name doesn't lie: it's all about dumplings in this bright room under bamboo lanterns. The dough pockets come steamed or pan-fried, in groups of 12 or 18, with fillings like lamb and coriander, ground pork and cabbage, sea whelk and leek, and some 30 other types. Bite into one and a hot shot of flavor erupts in your mouth. (☏312-799-1118; www.qxydumplings.com; 2002 S Wentworth Ave, Suite 103, Chinatown; mains $9-14; ⏱11:30am-9pm; Ⓜ Red Line to Cermak-Chinatown)

Pleasant House Pub

PUB FOOD $

9 ✖ MAP P134, F8

Follow your nose to Pleasant House, which bakes tall, fluffy, savory pies. Daily flavors include chicken and chutney, steak and ale, or kale and mushroom, made with produce the chefs grow themselves. The pub also serves excellent UK and local beers to accompany the food. Friday is a good day to visit, when there's a fish fry. (☏773-523-7437; www.pleasanthousepub.com; 2119 S Halsted St, Pilsen; mains $10.50-15; ⏱10am-10pm Tue-Thu, to midnight Fri & Sat, to 10pm Sun; 🛜; ☒8)

Don Pedro Carnitas

MEXICAN $

10 ✖ MAP P134, E7

At this no-frills meat den, a man with a machete salutes you at the front counter. He awaits your command to hack off pork pieces and then wraps the thick chunks with onion and cilantro in a warm tortilla. You then devour the tacos at the tables in back. Goat stew and tripe add to the carnivorous menu. Cash only. (1113 W 18th St, Pilsen; tacos $2.50; ⏱6am-6pm Mon-Thu, 5am-5pm Fri-Sun; Ⓜ Pink Line to 18th St)

Taqueria El Milagro   MEXICAN $

11 ⊗ MAP P134, C7

El Milagro is a classic. On one side it's a restaurant, with a cafeteria-style line for plates of beef stew simmering in tomato sauce or chicken in chocolate-y mole sauce. Mexican music plays above the clatter of locals hunkered down over their meals. On the other side it's a tortilla factory with a store to buy fresh packs of the goods. (☏312-433-7620; 1923 S Blue Island Ave, Pilsen; mains $3.50-7; ⏱8am-7pm Mon-Thu, 7:30am-8pm Fri & Sat, 7:30am-7pm Sun; Ⓜ Pink Line to 18th St)

Chiu Quon Bakery & Dim Sum   BAKERY $

12 ⊗ MAP P134, B5

For a cheap à la carte lunch in Chinatown, this bright bakery has fluffy BBQ pork buns, bite-sized egg custard tarts, coconut and winter melon pastries and some dim-sum fare (shrimp dumplings, taro cake, sticky rice roll, steamed egg custard *bao*). It's available to go, or to scarf down by the handful at the no-frills tables in back. Cash only. (☏312-808-1818; www.cqbakery.com; 2253 S Wentworth Ave, Chinatown; pastries & snacks $1-4; ⏱7am-10pm)

5 Rabanitos   MEXICAN $$

13 ⊗ MAP P134, B7

A storefront restaurant painted yellow, green and blue, 5 Rabanitos looks like any other taqueria on 18th St, except the chef learned his craft from renowned restaurateur Rick Bayless. Unusual spice combinations and addictive salsa and mole sauces make the dishes shine way beyond the norm. Try *torta ahogada*, a pork sandwich bathed in chili sauce. Several vegetarian options. BYOB. (☏312-285-2710; www.5rabanitos.com; 1758 W 18th St, Pilsen; mains $15-17; ⏱11am-9pm Tue-Thu, 11am-10pm Fri, 9am-10pm Sat, 9am-9pm Sun; 🖊; Ⓜ Pink Line to 18th St)

Drinking

La Catrina Cafe   CAFE

14 ⊖ MAP P134, E7

Activists, artists and students congregate here for the roomy window seats, soul-warming drinks and funky art exhibitions.

Chicago's Chinatown 🍴

Chicago's small but busy Chinatown is an easy 10-minute train ride from the Loop. Take the Red Line to the Cermak-Chinatown stop, which puts you between the neighborhood's two distinct parts: Chinatown Square (an enormous bi-level strip mall) unfurls to the north along Archer Ave, while Old Chinatown (the traditional retail area) stretches along Wentworth Ave to the south. Either zone allows you to graze through bakeries and shop for Hello Kitty trinkets.

It's a come-one, come-all kind of spot, prime for a Mexican hot chocolate, cinnamon-spiced coffee or Frida Kahlo–face cookie. A colorful mural marks the entrance. (📞312-434-4040; www.facebook.com/lacatrinacafeon18; 1011 W 18th St, Pilsen; ⏱7am-9pm Mon-Thu, 7am-6pm Fri, 8am-6pm Sat & Sun; 🛜; Ⓜ Pink Line to 18th St)

Moody Tongue   MICROBREWERY

15 🚇 MAP P134, F8

A crackling fire, stylish glassware and, most of all, sophisticated brews featuring culinary ingredients such as black truffle and Oaxacan chocolate make this hidden-in-plain-sight Pilsen taproom more suited to an intimate aperitif than a wild night with your beer buds. (📞312-600-5111; www.moodytongue.com; 2136 S Peoria St, Pilsen; ⏱5-10pm Wed, 5-11pm Thu, 5pm-midnight Fri, noon-midnight Sat, noon-9pm Sun; 🚌8)

Chicago Football

The Bears, Chicago's NFL team, tackle at **Soldier Field** (Map p134, E2; 📞847-615-2327; www.chicagobears.com; 1410 S Museum Campus Dr, Near South Side; 🚌146, 130) from September through January. Arrive early on game days and wander through the parking lots – you won't believe the elaborate tailgate feasts people cook up from the back of their cars.

Skylark   BAR

16 🚇 MAP P134, F8

The Skylark is a bastion for artsy guzzlers, who slouch into big booths sipping on strong drinks and eyeing the long room. They play pinball, snap pics in the photo booth and scarf down the kitchen's awesome tater tots. It's a good stop after the Pilsen gallery hop (a free arts event run by galleries, shops and studios). Cash only. (📞312-948-5275; www.skylarkchicago.com; 2149 S Halsted St, Pilsen; ⏱4pm-2am Sun-Fri, to 3am Sat; 🛜; 🚌8)

Entertainment

Thalia Hall   LIVE MUSIC

17 ⭐ MAP P134, D7

Midsize Thalia hosts a cool-cat slate of rock, alt-country, jazz and metal concerts in an ornate 1892 hall patterned after Prague's opera house. A gastropub on the 1st floor, cocktail bar in the basement and punk piano saloon in the adjacent carriage house invite lingering before and after shows. (📞312-526-3851; www.thaliahallchicago.com; 1807 S Allport St, Pilsen; Ⓜ Pink Line to 18th St)

Shopping

Pilsen Community Books   BOOKS

18 🅱 MAP P134, E7

Decorated with vintage typewriters and old card-catalog bureaus

ROBIN ALAM/ICON SPORTSWIRE VIA GETTY IMAGES ©

Chicago Bears play at Soldier Field

that serve as desks, this small store for new and used books charms. Sliding ladders provide access to the floor-to-ceiling bookshelves stacked with fiction, poetry, philosophy and lots of Spanish-language books. As part of the shop's community-focused mission, it gives free books to local schools. (www.pilsencommunity books.org; 1102 W 18th St, Pilsen; ☉11am-6pm Sun & Mon, to 9pm Tue-Sat; Ⓜ Pink Line to 18th St)

Pilsen Outpost ARTS & CRAFTS

19 🅐 MAP P134, B7

This compact artist-run gallery and shop sells distinctive silk-screened T-shirts, zines, cards, posters and small paintings on canvas. Everything is locally made. Staff are terrifically welcoming.

(📞773-830-4800; www.pilsenoutpost. com; 1637 W 18th St, Pilsen; ☉noon-8pm Wed-Fri, 11am-7pm Sat, 11am-5pm Sun; Ⓜ Pink Line to 18th St)

Knee Deep Vintage VINTAGE

Knee Deep (see 17 ✪ Map p134, D7) offers a trove of vintage clothing for men and women. Browse the racks past the 1970s feather-print dresses and 1960s Hawaiian-style shirts until you spot that perfect 1950s faux-leopard-fur coat. The owner stocks a quality selection, and prices are reasonable though not cheap. The shop is in the Thalia Hall building. (📞312-850-2510; www. kneedeepvintage.com; 1219 W 18th St, Pilsen; ☉noon-8pm Mon-Thu, 11am-8pm Fri & Sat, noon-6pm Sun; Ⓜ Pink Line to 18th St)

Worth a Trip 👓
Museum of Science & Industry

Geek out at the largest science museum in the Western Hemisphere. Highlights include a WWII German U-boat nestled in an underground display, the life-size shaft of a coal mine, and the Science Storms exhibit with a mock tornado and tsunami.

www.msichicago.org; 5700 S Lake Shore Dr, Hyde Park; adult/child $22/13

🕑9:30am-5:30pm Jun-Aug, shorter hours Sep-May

🚌6, 10 Ⓜ Metra Electric Line to 55th-56th-57th St

Level 1 & the Submarine

Level 1 holds the **U-boat**, which is pretty freaking impressive. It's given the Hollywood treatment with blue spotlights moving over it and dramatic music swelling in the background. An interactive kiosk lets you try to break codes. There's plenty more to see around the sub, but the highlight is going on board and touring the cramped quarters. Tours cost $18 extra ($14 for children); tickets are available at the exhibit-side kiosk (or at the main desk when you enter the museum). The **Space Center** with rockets and the *Apollo 8* lunar module, the **'fairy castle' dollhouse** and the **Farm Tech exhibit** with huge tractors to climb are other Level 1 highlights.

Levels 2 & 3

Level 2 rolls out lots of trains. **Science Storms** lets you conjure a mock tornado and simulate a tsunami rolling toward you. Or submerge into the realistic shaft of a **coal mine** ($12 extra for adults, $9 for children). The **baby chick hatchery** is also on this floor.

Level 3 hangs cool old **German dive bombers** and **English Spitfires** from the ceiling. *You! The Experience* has a giant 3-D heart to walk through and the infamous body slices (cadavers displayed in half-inch-thick pieces) that have been scaring kids for decades.

Outdoor Sights

The museum's main building served as the Palace of Fine Arts at the landmark 1893 World's Expo, which was set in surrounding **Jackson Park** (6401 S Stony Island Ave, Woodlawn; 🚆6, Ⓜ Metra Electric Line to 59th or 63rd St). When you've had your fill at the museum, the park makes an excellent setting to recuperate.

★ Top Tips

o In summer and during popular exhibits lines can be long. Purchase tickets online in advance.

o Kids 10 and under love the hands-on Idea Factory on Level 1; big kids get stoked for the flight simulators ($6 to $8 extra) on Level 3.

✕ Take a Break

Medici (📞773-667-7394; www.medici57.com; 1327 E 57th St, Hyde Park; mains $9-16; ⏰7am-10pm Mon-Thu, 7am-11pm Fri, 9am-11pm Sat, 9am-10pm Sun; 🛜🍽👪; 🚆6, Ⓜ Metra Electric Line to 55th-56th-57th) whips up pizzas and bakery goods; it's about a half-mile walk away.

Cove Lounge (📞773-684-1013; www.thecovelounge.com; 1750 E 55th St, Hyde Park; ⏰11am-2am Sun-Fri, to 3am Sat; 🚆6, Ⓜ Metra Electric Line to 55th-56th-57th St) is a neighborhood bar with a swell jukebox.

Worth a Trip 👀
Robie House

Robie House is one of the most famous dwellings in the world. Designed by Frank Lloyd Wright, it's the masterpiece of his Prairie style, and it is often listed among the most important structures in American architecture. The look is meant to reflect the Midwest's landscape – low-slung with long horizontal lines and lots of earth colors.

📞 312-994-4000

www.flwright.org

5757 S Woodlawn Ave, Hyde Park

adult/child $18/15

🕐 10:30am-3pm Thu-Mon

🚌 6, Ⓜ Metra Electric Line to 59th St

Robie Family History

Frederick C Robie, a forward-thinking businessman who dealt in early auto machinery, was only 28 years old when he commissioned Wright to build a modern house for his family. Wright designed it between 1908 and 1909 but wasn't around for most of the construction, as he had moved to Europe with his mistress by then. The Robies moved in in 1910, but after 14 months, financial and marital problems forced them to sell the house.

Interior & Tours

The house cost about $60,000 to build – furniture, light fixtures and 174 art glass windows included. The corner lot on which Robie House sits is three times as long as it is wide, which prompted Wright to envision the home as a set of long, narrow rectangles.

Extensive work has been completed restoring the interior to Wright's original vision. Note how the furniture repeats the building's forms, and how the colors link to the autumnal prairie palette. Docents tell the story during one-hour house tours, run roughly every half-hour Thursday to Monday from June through October, and hourly otherwise.

Saving Robie House

After the Robies, the house was sold a few times – finally in 1926 to the Chicago Theological Seminary, for use as a dormitory. The seminary twice announced plans to raze the structure and build a bigger dorm: in 1941, when a letter-writing campaign saved the house; and again in 1957, when 90-year-old Frank Lloyd Wright himself showed up to ask that it be preserved. That same year, Robie House became the first building declared a Chicago landmark.

★ Top Tips

o Advance tickets are highly recommended; call or go online. There's a small surcharge for reservations.

o The small gift shop has Prairie-design coasters, night lights, candleholders and more. Proceeds support ongoing preservation efforts here.

✕ Take a Break

The bustling **Plein Air Cafe** (☏773-966-7531; www.pleinaircafe.com; 5751 S Woodlawn Ave, Hyde Park; mains $7-11; ⏰7am-8pm Mon-Fri, 8am-6pm Sat & Sun; 🚍6, Ⓜ Metra Electric Line to 59th St) sits next door in the Seminary Co-op Bookstore.

Jimmy's Woodlawn Tap (☏773-643-5516; 1172 E 55th St, Hyde Park; ⏰10:30am-2am Mon-Fri, 11am-3am Sat, 11am-2am Sun; 🚍6, Ⓜ Metra Electric Line to 55th-56th-57th St), about a half-mile away, is brilliant for a beer and burger.

Survival Guide

Water Tower (p76) DAVE NEWMAN/SHUTTERSTOCK ©

Before You Go

Book Your Stay

o Accommodations will likely be your biggest expense in Chicago.

o The best digs are wired-up boutique hotels set in architectural landmarks.

o Several independent hostels have popped up in fun, outlying neighborhoods such as Wicker Park and Wrigleyville.

o Enormous business hotels cater to conventioneers in the Loop and Near North.

o Low-key B&Bs are in Wicker Park and Lake View and can be cheaper than hotels.

Useful Websites

Lonely Planet (www. lonelyplanet.com/ hotels) Recommendations and bookings.

Chicago Bed & Breakfast Association (www.chicago-bed-breakfast.com) Represents around 11 properties.

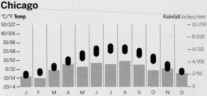

Chicago

When to Go

o **Winter (Dec–Feb)** Chicago twinkles with holiday festivities in December. Cold-weather bargains abound in winter.

o **Spring (Mar–May)** Gradually warmer weather brings shoulder season discounts.

o **Summer (Jun–Aug)** Peak season, when it's warm and festivals rock the town.

o **Autumn (Sep–Nov)** September and October are good months for decent weather and prices.

Hotel Tonight (www. hoteltonight.com) National discounter with last-minute deals; book via the free app.

Choose Chicago (www.choosechicago. com) Options from the city's official website.

Best Budget

Found Hotel (www. foundhotels.com) Part hostel, part hotel with good-time common areas.

Wicker Park Inn (www.wickerparkinn. com) Cozy B&B in the thick of Wicker Park's social scene.

Holiday Jones (www. holidayjones.com) Good-value, off-the-beaten-path hostel with a sense of humor.

Freehand Chicago (www.freehandhotels. com/chicago) Super-hip hostel-hotel hybrid with spiffy, high-tech dorms.

HI-Chicago (www. hichicago.org) You can't beat the Loop location and free city tours.

Best Midrange

Hampton Inn Chicago Downtown/N Loop (www.hamptonchicago.

com) The chain's much-loved amenities in retro, charismatic environs.

Majestic Hotel (www.majestic-chicago.com) Handsome, English-manor-like property near the lake.

Hotel Lincoln (www.jdvhotels.com) Fun, from 'wall of bad art' kitsch to pedicab service.

Willows Hotel (www.willowshotelchicago.com) Peachy rooms fill the dapper little property.

Moxy Chicago Downtown (www.moxyhotels.marriott.com) Compact rooms and communal areas that party hard.

Best Top End

Viceroy Chicago (www.viceroyhotelsandresorts.com) Chicago's newest luxury hotel wows with plush rooms, gracious amenities and attentive service.

Waldorf Astoria (www.waldorfastoriachicagohotel.com) A name synonymous with classic hotel opulence lives up to its five-star reputation.

Fairmont (www.

fairmont.com/chicago) Top-shelf accommodations a stone's throw from Millennium Park with unbeatable views.

Peninsula Chicago (www.peninsula.com) One of the city's most prestigious luxe hotels.

Arriving in Chicago

O'Hare Airport

Seventeen miles northwest of the Loop, **O'Hare International Airport** (ORD; ☎ 800-832-6352; www.flychicago.com/ohare; 10000 W O'Hare Ave) is the headquarters for United Airlines and a hub for American Airlines. Most non-US airlines and international flights use Terminal 5; domestic terminals are 1, 2 and 3. ATMs and currency exchanges are available throughout. Wi-fi is free, but slow.

Midway Airport

Eleven miles southwest of the Loop, **Midway International Airport** (MDW; ☎ 773-838-0600; www.flychicago.com/midway; 5700 S Cicero

Ave. Clearing) has three concourses: A, B and C. Southwest Airlines uses B; most other airlines go out of A. There's a currency exchange in A and ATMs throughout. Wi-fi is free, but slow.

Union Station

Grand, Doric-columned **Union Station** (www.chicagounionstation.com; 225 S Canal St; Ⓜ Blue Line to Clinton) is the city's rail hub, located at the Loop's western edge. Amtrak (www.amtrak.com) has more connections here than anywhere else in the country.

Getting Around

Bicycle

o Chicago is a cycling-savvy city with a well-used bike-share program. **Divvy** (www.divvybikes.com) has some 5800 sky-blue bikes at 580 stations.

o The $15 day pass allows unlimited rides in a 24-hour period, up to three hours each. A $3 single-ride pass gets

30 minutes. Both can be purchased at station kiosks or via the Divvy app. Rates rise fast if you don't dock the bike in your allotted time.

o Having the Divvy app makes life much easier for finding docks, checking availability and paying.

o Bike rentals for longer rides (with accoutrements such as helmets and locks) start at around $8 per hour. Try **Bike & Roll** (Map p44, F2; 312-729-1000; www. bikechicago.com; 239 E Randolph St; tours adult/child from $45/35; 9am-7pm; M Brown, Orange, Green, Purple, Pink Line to Washington/Wabash) or **Bobby's Bike Hike** (Map p58, G3; 312-245-9300; www. bobbysbikehike.com; 540 N Lake Shore Dr, Streeterville; per hr/day from $8/27, tours $38-70; 8:30am-8pm Mon-Fri, 8am-8pm Sat & Sun Jun-Aug, 9am-7pm Mar-May & Sep-Nov; M Red Line to Grand). They also rent children's bikes, and offer discounts if you book online.

Bus

o City buses operate from early morning until late evening.

o The fare is $2.25 ($2.50 if you want a transfer). You can use a Ventra Card (a recharge-able fare card that you buy at L stations) or pay the driver with exact change.

o Buses are particularly useful for reaching the Museum Campus, the Museum of Science & Industry and Lincoln Park's zoo.

Taxi

o Taxis are plentiful in the Loop, north to Andersonville and northwest to Wicker Park/Bucktown. Hail them with a wave of the hand.

o Fares are meter-based and start at $3.25 when you get into the cab, then it's $2.25 per mile. The first extra passenger costs $1; extra passengers after that are 50¢ apiece. Add 10% to 15% for a tip.

o All major companies accept credit cards.

o The ridesharing companies **Uber** (www. uber.com), **Lyft** (www. lyft.com) and **Via** (www. ridewithvia.com) are also popular in Chicago. They can be a bit cheaper than taxis.

Train

o The L (a system of elevated and subway trains) is fast, frequent and will get you to most sights and neighbor-hoods.

o Two of the eight color-coded lines – the Red Line, and the Blue Line to O'Hare airport – operate 24 hours a day. The other lines run from roughly 4am to 1am daily, departing every 10 minutes or so.

o The standard fare is $3 (except from O'Hare airport, where it costs $5) and includes two transfers. Enter the turnstile using a Ventra Ticket, which is sold from vending machines at train stations.

o Unlimited ride passes (one-/three-/seven-day $10/20/28) are another handy option. Get them at train stations and drugstores.

o For maps and route planning, check the website of the **Chicago Transit Authority** (www. transitchicago.com). The 'Trackers' section tells you when the next train or bus is due to arrive at your station.

Essential Information

Accessible Travel

o Most museums and major sights are wheelchair accessible, as are most large hotels and restaurants.

o All city buses are wheelchair accessible, but about one-third of L stations are not.

o **Easy Access Chicago** (www.easyaccess chicago.org) is a free resource that lists museums, tours, restaurants and lodgings, and provides mobility, vision and hearing accessibility information for each place.

o The **Mayor's Office for People with Disabilities** (www.cityofchicago.org/disabilities) can answer questions about the availability of services in the city.

Business Hours

Typical normal opening times are as follows:

Banks & businesses 9am to 5pm Monday to Friday

Bars 5pm to 2am (to 3am on Saturday); some licensed until 4am (to 5am on Saturday)

Nightclubs 10pm to 4am; often closed Monday through Wednesday

Restaurants Breakfast 7am or 8am to 11am, lunch 11am or 11:30am to 2:30pm, dinner 5pm or 6pm to 10pm Sunday to Thursday, to 11pm or midnight Friday and Saturday

Shops 11am to 7pm Monday to Saturday, noon to 6pm Sunday

Discount Cards

o The **Go Chicago Card** (www.smartdestinations.com/chicago) lets you visit an unlimited number of attractions for a flat fee, including architecture cruises, the Navy Pier Ferris wheel and all major museums. It's good for one, two, three or five consecutive days. The company also offers a three-, four- or five-choice **Explorer Pass** where you pick among 29 options for sights.

o **CityPass** (www.citypass.com/chicago) gives access to five of the city's top draws, including the Art Institute, Shedd Aquarium and Willis Tower, over nine consecutive days. It's less flexible than Go Chicago's pass, but cheaper for those wanting a more leisurely sightseeing pace.

Electricity

Type A
120V/60Hz

Type B
120V/60Hz

Money-Saving Tips

o Although the airports have currency exchange bureaus, better rates can usually be obtained in the city.

o Buy a rechargeable Ventra Card if you're going to use the L train more than a few times. They're available at any train station, are more convenient than disposable fare tickets, and save around 75¢ per ride.

Emergencies

Nonemergency police matters	☎ 311
Police, fire, ambulance	☎ 911

Money

ATMs

o ATMs are widely available 24/7 at banks, airports and convenience stores.

o Most ATMs link into worldwide networks (Plus, Cirrus, Exchange etc).

o ATMs typically charge a service fee of $3 or more per transaction, and your home bank may impose additional charges.

Credit Cards

Major credit cards are almost universally accepted. In fact, it's next to impossible to rent a car or make hotel or ticket reservations without one. Visa and MasterCard are the most widely accepted.

Tipping

Tipping isn't optional. Only withhold tips in cases of outrageously bad service.

Airport & hotel porters $2 per bag, minimum per cart $5

Bartenders 15% to 20% per round, minimum $1/2 per drink for standard drinks/specialty cocktails

Housekeeping staff $2 to $5 daily

Restaurant servers 18% to 20% (unless gratuity already on bill)

Taxi drivers 10% to 15% (round up to next dollar)

Parking valets $2 to $5 when handed back the keys

Public Holidays

Banks, schools, offices and most shops close on these days:

New Year's Day January 1

Martin Luther King Jr Day Third Monday in January

Presidents' Day Third Monday in February

Pulaski Day First Monday in March (observed mostly by city offices)

Memorial Day Last Monday in May

Independence Day July 4

Labor Day First Monday in September

Columbus Day Second Monday in October

Veteran's Day November 11

Thanksgiving Day Fourth Thursday in November

Christmas Day December 25

Safe Travel

o You've probably heard about Chicago's high murder rate, but it's mostly concentrated in a handful of far west and far south neigborhoods.

o Overall, serious crime in Chicago has been dropping in recent years, and major tourist areas are all reasonably safe.

o You should still take normal, big-city precautions, especially solo at night. Many crimes involve cell phone theft, so be subtle when using yours.

Telephone

In Chicago, you will always dial 11 numbers: 1 + the three-digit area code + the seven-digit local number.

Cell Phones

International travelers can use local SIM cards in a smartphone provided it is unlocked. Alternatively, you can buy a cheap US phone and load it up with prepaid minutes.

Phonecards

Private prepaid phonecards are available from convenience stores, supermarkets and pharmacies. AT&T

sells a reliable card that is widely available.

Toilets

Public toilets are few and far between. There are some at **Millennium Park** (Map p44, F3; 312-742-1168; www.millenniumpark.org; 201 E Randolph St; 6am-11pm; ; Brown, Orange, Green, Purple, Pink Line to Washington/Wabash) near Pritzker Pavilion and at **Maggie Daley Park** (Map p44, G3; www.maggiedaleypark.com; 337 E Randolph St; 6am-11pm; ; Brown, Orange, Green, Purple, Pink Line to Washington/Wabash) at the field house, but they aren't always open. There are limited facilities at the **Chicago Cultural Center** (Map p44, E2; 312-744-6630; www.chicagoculturalcenter.org; 78 E Washington St;

10am-7pm Mon-Fri, to 5pm Sat & Sun; Brown, Orange, Green, Purple, Pink Line to Washington/Wabash), by the Landmark Gallery. The Loop's **Target** (Map p44, D3; www.target.com; 1 S State St; 7am-10pm Mon-Fri, from 8am Sat & Sun; ; Brown, Orange, Green, Purple, Pink Line to Madison) store is another option.

Tourist Information

Choose Chicago (www.choosechicago.com) is the city's official tourism site, with loads of information online.

Visas

Generally not required for stays of up to 90 days; check www.travel.state.gov for details.

Dos & Don'ts

Smoking Don't smoke in restaurants or bars: Chicago is smoke-free by law in those venues.

Dining Most people eat dinner between 6pm and 8pm (a bit later if dining out).

On escalators Stand to the right on the escalators; walk on the left.

Behind the Scenes

Send Us Your Feedback

We love to hear from travelers – your comments help make our books better. We read every word, and we guarantee that your feedback goes straight to the authors. Visit **lonelyplanet.com/contact** to submit your updates and suggestions.

Note: We may edit, reproduce and incorporate your comments in Lonely Planet products such as guidebooks, websites and digital products, so let us know if you don't want your comments reproduced or your name acknowledged. For a copy of our privacy policy visit lonelyplanet.com/privacy.

Acknowledgements

Cover photograph: Flamingo, by Alexander Calder, outside Kluczynski Federal Building, Susanne Kremer/© 2018 Calder Foundation, New York/Copyright Agency, Australia

Ali's Thanks

My thanks to Jo Wright, Zina Alam and Igor Enin for looking after my furchildren; to Karla Zimmerman, Cate Huguelet, Trisha Ping and Krystyn Wells for Chi-town inspiration and socializing; and to Laura and Karla Ruiz for their hospitality and local recommendations — and especially to their dog Bruno, who's a very good boy indeed.

Karla's Thanks

Deep appreciation to all of the locals who spilled the beans on their favorite places. Special thanks to Kari Lydersen, Ali Lemer, Lisa Dunford and Chris and Kevin Kohl. Thanks most to Eric Markowitz, the world's best partner-for-life, who kindly indulges my beer and donut fixations. You top my Best List.

This Book

This 4th edition of Lonely Planet's *Pocket Chicago* guidebook was curated by Ali Lemer and researched and written by Ali and Karla Zimmerman. This guidebook was produced by the following:

Destination Editor
Trisha Ping

Senior Product Editors
Elizabeth Jones, Victoria Smith

Regional Senior Cartographers Alison Lyall, Corey Hutchison

Product Editors Fergus O'Shea, Daniel Bolger

Book Designer Ania Bartoszek

Assisting Editors
Michelle Bennett, Victoria Harrison, Jennifer Hattam, Gabrielle Stefanos

Cover Researcher
Meri Blazevski

Thanks to Stephen Andrew, Carol Collins, Fergal Condon, Gwen Cotter, Frank V Coulter, Simon Fowler, Evan Godt, Cate Huguelet, Sandie Kestell, Amy Lynch, Genna Patterson, Alison Ridgway, Claire Rourke, Angela Tinson, Amanda Williamson

Index

See also separate subindexes for:

🍴 **Eating 157**

🍷 **Drinking 158**

✪ **Entertainment 159**

🔒 **Shopping 159**

⊗ Eating

Our Writers

Ali Lemer
Ali has been a Lonely Planet writer and editor sinc 2007, and has authored guidebooks and travel ar cles on Russia, Germany, NYC, Chicago, Los Ange Melbourne, Bali, Hawaii, Japan and Scotland. A na New Yorker, Ali has also lived in Melbourne, Chica Prague and England, and has traveled extensively around Europe, North America, Oceania and Asia

Karla Zimmerman
Karla lives in Chicago, where she eats donuts, ye at the Cubs, and writes stuff for books, magazine and websites when she's not doing the first two things. She has contributed to 70-plus Lonely Pla guidebooks and travel anthologies covering dest tions in Europe, Asia, Africa, North America and t Caribbean. To learn more, follow her on Instagra and Twitter (@karlazimmerman).

Published by Lonely Planet Global Limited
CRN 554153
4th edition – Jan 2020
ISBN 978 1 78701 409 1
© Lonely Planet 2020 Photographs © as indicated 2020
10 9 8 7 6 5 4 3 2 1
Printed in Singapore